JEET KUNE DO
A CORE STRUCTURE TRAINING MANUAL

Dave Carnell

THE CROWOOD PRESS

First published in 2008 by
The Crowood Press Ltd
Ramsbury, Marlborough
Wiltshire SN8 2HR

www.crowood.com

British Library Cataloguing-in-Publication Data
A catalogue record for this book is available from the British Library.

ISBN 978 1 84797 003 9

Disclaimer
Please note that the author and the publisher of this book are not responsible
in any manner whatsoever for any damage or injury of any kind that may
result from practising, or applying, the principles, ideas, techniques and/or
following the instructions/information described in this publication. Since the
physical activities described in this book may be too strenuous in nature for
some readers to engage in safely, it is essential that a doctor be consulted
before undertaking training.

Designed and typeset by Focus Publishing,
11a St Botolph's Road, Sevenoaks, Kent TN13 3AJ

Printed and bound in Malaysia by Times Offset (M) Sdn Bhd

Contents

Foreword *by Cass Magda*

Ever since 1984, when I first met Dave Carnell, I was impressed. Here was a man with a burning desire to learn, grow and go to the next level. Since that moment I have watched and participated in Dave's growth into a superb Jeet Kune Do exponent and teacher. He has a keen sense of observation and analysis which he has applied constantly over the years and is now generously sharing his knowledge with all those who walk the JKD path.

There are many training ideas and explanations given about Bruce Lee's JKD that are based on perception and not reality. One such perception is that JKD is a do-it-yourself, put-together 'best of all styles' martial art. The reality is that you cannot really 'know' an art without understanding its design and structure. Every martial art has a structure, whether it is Western boxing, muay thai, Brazilian jiu jitsu, karate, escrima, silat or judo. To know JKD then, you must know and practise its unique structure. The understanding encompasses physics, anatomy, timing, rhythm and specific principles such as economy of motion, non-telegraphic motion and understanding how to use body mechanics to hit very hard.

Anyone who really gets deep into JKD soon realizes it is the little things in the structure that make all the difference in the performance. Details such as how to align the hips when hitting, or learning to push yourself into position rather than stepping, are intimately connected to understanding its structure. Knowing the structure allows you to read your opponent's moves and analyze his strengths and weaknesses. Mastering the structure makes for a tight defence and instantaneous response in counter-attack. It allows your body to respond effortlessly to the moment to moment of fighting and keeps you emotionally cool to conserve energy. In JKD, we learn this structure and internalize it so our moves flow out of our unconscious mind. As we practise longer, we develop and customize it, making it unique to ourselves.

To repeat a phrase that Bruce Lee loved from the German philosopher Goethe, 'knowing is not enough, we must apply.' Many who practise JKD sometimes gloss over the very things that would make them great. It seems 'knowing' is enough for them. Those few who are interested in the details of 'applying' will find this book a valuable reference that they will go back to again and again.

Cass Magda
Los Angeles, California.

4

Foreword *by Tim Tackett*

It is a great pleasure for me to write a foreword to a Jeet Kune Do book by Dave Carnell. I first met Dave around twenty years ago when I did my first JKD seminar in the United Kingdom. At that time Dave was a Wing Chun practitioner who had a keen interest in learning Jeet Kune Do. Learning JKD in the UK at that time was extremely difficult as you either had to go to the United States to train or attend as many seminars as you could in Europe. Dave made every effort to learn when and where he could. Every time I saw Dave he had got better and better. Sometimes I will teach something at a seminar and if I go back a few years later, the instructors and their students still can't do it. This is because many people will see a technique, work on it a little and then think they can do it in combat but really have no clue. This was not true of Dave. Every time I saw him he got better and once he was able to open up a school and do martial arts full time, he got better still.

The most important aspect of being a JKD teacher is not how good you are but how good your students are. I've had the pleasure of teaching instructors that are under Dave as well as many of his students and I have found all of them to be excellent teachers, students and most important of all, good people.

Dave knows JKD and can teach JKD and this is rare indeed. I truly feel that Dave Carnell has become one of the best Jeet Kune Do teachers that I have seen. I am very happy that he has finally decided to share his JKD knowledge with those who have not been able to train with him.

Tim Tackett
Redlands, California

Dedication

To the spirit of Sijo Bruce Lee.

To Si-Gung Dan Inosanto, who inspired me to take the JKD path and still inspires me to this day.

To my Sifu Cass Magda, who has been with me every step of the way.

To my partner Keely for her support, encouragement and love.

Acknowledgements

My special thanks to Carol Woods for sitting with me into the early hours of the morning both typing and proof reading. Without her help I have no doubt that this book would never have been finished; to Keely Woods and Jean Hanley for stepping in at the darkest hour to keep the whole process going to plan; to Simon McGovern for his creativity and artwork; to my old friend Andrew Staton, a man with a huge heart whose photographic skills are exceptional; to my loyal students John Boote, Tom Wood, Steve Wan, Simon McGovern and Neal Haxton, for helping me with the demonstrations in the photographs.

My Sifu, Cass Magda, has always provided me with guidance for which I am eternally grateful. Also, my thanks go to Tim Tackett and Chris Kent for helping me along the 'Martial Way.'

My special thanks go to Carlos Lemos Jr, my Brazilian Jiu Jitsu master and my friend.

For sharing their knowledge with me, my sincerest thanks go to all of the following people, whose understanding of the art has influenced and inspired my growth and development as a practitioner and a teacher: Bob Bremer, Ted Wong, Richard Bustillo, Jerry Poteet, Pete Jacobs, Herb Jackson, Larry Hartsell, Steve Golden, Dan Lee, Ted Lucay Lucay, James Demille, Taky Kimura and Del Pollard.

Fig 1. Back row: John Boote, Dave Carnell, Tom Wood;
front row: Steve Wan, Simon McGovern, Neal Haxton

Preface – About the Author

Dave Carnell began his training in martial arts at an early age, dabbling in judo with his friends. He returned to the martial arts as a teenager, inspired by the movies and television shows of the 1970s. This was when he saw his first glimpse of the impressive Bruce Lee.

His first serious training was at the local Lau-Gar Kung Fu School. This lasted approximately twelve months. Dave then started to train in a system called Chi-San-Tao which was a blend of styles which included Wing Chun gung fu. He knew that this was the same art that Bruce Lee had gained his foundation in. With his interest in Wing Chun growing, Dave decided that it was this system that he would like to study in greater depth. He met and trained with many of the UK's top Wing Chun sifus of the time, including John Darwin, Danny Conner, Simon Lau and Samuel Kwok. Dave trained extensively with Samuel Kwok and was instrumental in the development and production of his book *Path to Wing Chun*, becoming one of the first instructors for the Samuel Kwok Martial Arts Association. Dave was in turn introduced to Samuel's teacher Ip Chun, the eldest son of Ip Man, who was Bruce Lee's Wing Chun teacher.

During this period, Dave was studying on a three-year college foundation course in art and design, which was to lead onto a degree. However, he never went on to do the degree, instead choosing to be a professional martial arts teacher, opening up his school full time.

In 1984, whilst training and researching with various Wing Chun teachers, Dave came to realize that each sifu had their own individual interpretation of the art and he wanted to find out more about this idea of individual perspectives. During this time, Dan Inosanto came to give a seminar in London. Dave attended the seminar hoping to find another angle on the Wing Chun system. This was a turning point in his martial arts. It was a first-hand introduction to Jeet Kune Do and the many other arts that Guro Dan was into at the time. In his own words, Dave was 'just blown away'. His eyes were opened to the speed, skill and sophistication of not only Dan himself but his young assistants at that time, Cass Magda and Chris Kent.

After this first seminar, Dave continued to attend most of Inosanto's seminars, including those of his students Larry Hartsell, Chris Kent, Cass Magda and Tim Tackett. He also attended other first-generation Bruce Lee students' seminars, including ones by Dan Lee, Ted Wong, Richard Bustillo and Jerry Poteet. This continued until Dave was inviting most of these people to do seminars in his own school and was in return invited to train in the USA.

Dave continued to train on a private basis with Cass Magda. In 1990 he became authorized to teach JKD, Kali and Silat. During this time Dave became a JKD advisor and columnist for several years with *Martial Arts Illustrated* magazine, producing and compiling the book *What's in a Name – Jeet Kune Do* for MAI publications. Dave was also the technical advisor on the DVD *Bruce Lee – Martial Arts Master*, which led to him being introduced to many of Bruce Lee's friends and students from the US. He spent many hours with them compiling and cross-referencing material and training methods to get the full picture of Jeet Kune Do.

Over many years of training, Dave has become a senior instructor for Cass Magda's MI Association and supervising instructor for the UK, with branches throughout the country. As director of the Impact Martial Arts Academy, he is now a sought-after Instructor on the seminar circuit, teaching throughout the UK and across Europe and America. Dave was the first person to take Jeet Kune Do to Poland, appearing on prime time television to demonstrate the art.

Dave still continues to train and learn new aspects of the martial arts with his current interest being the grappling range. His most recent achievements include being awarded his purple belt in Gracie Barra Brazilian jiu jitsu under Carlos Lemos Jr and receiving his Diploma in Sports Psychology.

Introduction – About the Book

I always knew that when the time was right I would write this book. After thirty-two years in the martial arts I feel is time to share my understanding, development and growth in the art and science of Jeet Kune Do.

This book is the result of many years of training, research and cross-referencing of material that I have learned, sometimes also interviewing and plain old 'hanging out' with a lot of Bruce Lee's students from the Oakland, Seattle and Los Angeles periods of his martial arts development. From this I have put together an overview of the structure of Jeet Kune Do. Although this book is primarily geared toward the beginner and intermediate student, I am sure it will be of interest to the seasoned practitioner as well.

Over the years I have come to realize that Jeet Kune Do is not just the picking and choosing of different techniques, the so-called 'best of the best', to make your own martial art. It has its own unique system, with a core foundation of a set of basic tools that the student can use to develop and grow.

Included in the book is a breakdown of the Bai-Jong On-Guard stance. Within this stance are the keys to Jeet Kune Do's attack and defence system. The different types of footwork are included that bring the stance alive and makes it totally mobile. Some of the most important attacking weapons are broken down in detail, and an explanation given of why these basic tools form the backbone of Jeet Kune Do's attack.

The various components of this structure fit together to allow it to function in the most efficient and alive manner. Practising the structure will give you built-in habits that you will use in a fighting situation; once internalized, it will free up the mind so that you can fit in with an opponent.

My sifu, Cass Magda, likes to use the analogy of Jeet Kune Do as a speedboat: slick, fast and designed for speed. If the speedboat is loaded up with too much cargo it may carry the load successfully, but is it still a speedboat following its original design? Sitting heavy in the water, it will move sluggishly as it tries to overcome the extra weight. It is not designed to carry a heavy cargo and therefore the boat is weighed down and loses its purpose.

Here then is a teaching manual and reference book of the core principles and structure of the art, which will guide you on your journey to self-discovery,. This book is also about helping you to use this material to reach your genetic potential, as Bruce Lee did to develop his. By using the guidelines within, you will adhere to the original design and purpose of Jeet Kune Do.

1 History and Philosophy

Bruce Lee

Bruce Lee Jun Fan was born in San Francisco on 27 November, 1940. His father was an actor in the Chinese Opera, which at the time was travelling on tour in the USA. The name Bruce was given to him by the doctor at the hospital where he was born although his mother called him 'Jun Fan', which means 'return again'. The surname Li was written as the English 'Lee' on his birth certificate.

In 1941 the Li family returned to Hong Kong. During his childhood Bruce appeared in no fewer than eighteen Hong Kong-produced movies. At his ninth birthday party he was introduced to William Cheung, a young martial artist who was receiving gung fu lessons from the legendary gung fu master Yip Man of the Wing Chun school. Bruce persuaded his mother to give him money for lessons, claiming that he was bullied at school and that martial arts would be a good form of self-defence. Around this time, Bruce and William joined a street gang called the 'Junction Street 8 Tigers', which was often in trouble with the police.

Hoping to instil some discipline into Bruce, brother Edward got him involved in the school boxing programme at St Francis Xavier Catholic School. Bruce showed some potential and was entered into the inter-school boxing match against rival school King George V. After progressing through three fights in the tournament, Bruce faced the defending champion in the final. He proceeded to straight blast his opponent and was duly crowned the 1958 high school boxing champion. Bruce's other passion was dancing, and he also became the cha-cha-cha champion of Hong Kong around this time.

Bruce became involved in rooftop fights against other styles of gung fu. These challenge matches led to further trouble with the police and resulted in him leaving Hong Kong to reclaim his US citizenship in 1959.

After a short stay in San Francisco teaching cha-cha-cha to the general public, he moved up to Seattle to enrol at the Edison Technical College. One of his first Wing Chun gung fu demonstrations was at the 1959 Seattle 'Seafair' exhibition. Jesse Glover, who was in the crowd at that time, sought out Bruce for lessons, and eventually became Bruce's first student and good friend. Jesse was already a black belt in judo and he showed Bruce a few throws. Bruce soon had a small group of students meeting at various locations in Seattle, including local parking lots and sports fields. The 'school' later moved to a more permanent location in the basement of Taky Kimura's supermarket. This became known as the Jun Fan Gung Fu Institute and is still run by Taky Kimura and his son to this day.

Around this time Bruce was teaching the original art of Wing Chun gung fu, which gave him some of the principles on which his future growth was based. It gave him an economical structure, directness and emphasis on sensitivity, which he supplemented with elements of other Chinese arts. He was fascinated by the stories of the ancient Chinese gung fu masters and he learnt and demonstrated forms from Praying Mantis, Southern Mantis, Wing Chun, Jeet Kune, Fu-Jow and Crane style of Gung Fu. He also had a collection of books on various styles of martial arts, including Hung-Gar, Choy-Li-Fut and tai chi. Even at this early stage Bruce envisioned a superior gung fu system.

In 1961 Bruce enrolled at the University of Washington. He continued to teach his gung fu classes, attracting students from the university, among them his future wife Linda Emery.

His existing method of fighting was close-in, so he researched and experimented with more long-range tools including some kicks from northern gung fu styles. He started to change things slightly to accommodate larger Western opponents. Only small changes were made at first; for example, he changed the angles of his chi-sau (sticking hands) to create more pressure – what he called 'flowing energy'. There were modifications to the stance and footwork, and he also included some of the leg reaps and throws that he learnt from Jesse Glover.

He was greatly influenced by the Eastern philosophies of taoism and zen, and while at university would spend his spare time in the Chinese philosophy section of the library. He was especially taken with the aphorisms that related to his gung fu, blending these into explanations of gung fu techniques.

Whilst teaching in Seattle he received an invitation from James Lee (no relation) to visit him in Oakland. James was a Sil-Lum gung fu teacher who had heard of Bruce Lee's skill and wanted to check him out. Bruce was excited that word was getting out about his skill and the art of Wing Chun, although he now referred to his art as non-classical gung fu. The following week Bruce dropped by and spent the weekend with James at his home. It seems that they had a great deal in common and the foundation was laid for a strong friendship to develop. James introduced Bruce to weight training for martial arts and he had developed a lot of training devices which he kept in his garage and shared with Bruce. James also had his own martial arts book publishing company and had written several books on the martial arts. Bruce was impressed with James's work and it was James who encouraged Bruce to write a book on gung fu.

In 1963 Bruce's first book was published by James Lee entitled *Chinese Gung Fu: the Philosophical Art of Self Defence*. James Lee was also responsible for introducing Bruce to Kempo Karate legend Ed Parker, who was very impressed with Bruce's skill, inviting him to do a demonstration at the Long Beach Karate International Tournament in August 1964. That same month Bruce married Linda and moved into James Lee's home in Oakland, California. James and Bruce opened a second Jun Fan Gung Fu Institute, leaving Taky Kimura in charge of the Seattle school.

In January of 1965 Bruce's training was rudely interrupted by a group of Chinese gung fu men who represented the Chinese community of San Francisco. After entering the school they demanded that Bruce stop teaching non-Chinese or they would be forced to close him down, issuing a challenge to Bruce to fight the leader of the Chinese delegation, a man called Wong Jak Man. Bruce was fuming and said that he would fight him right now without any rules. The fight only lasted a few minutes, ending with Bruce chasing his opponent, striking him on the back of the head and then dragging him to the ground forcing him to stop. After the fight Bruce noticed that he was unusually winded and that his hands were painful from straight blasting the back of his opponent's head. He felt that although he had won the fight, it was not a good performance because he had relentlessly stuck to the Wing Chun pattern of chain punching. Over time, Bruce re-evaluated his training methods as he began to lose faith in the old classical styles of gung fu and started to develop a more athletic way of training based more on conditioning and fitness. His training methods became more like those of a Western boxer, retaining only certain elements of his Wing Chun gung fu.

In March 1966 Bruce and his family left Oakland for Los Angeles to develop his television career. Dan Inosanto had been introduced to Bruce in 1964 and had been the fall guy for Bruce in demonstrations before the famous Long Beach demonstration. The third Jun Fan Gung Fu Institute was eventually set up at 628 College Street in Los Angeles's China town. A greater emphasis was placed on conditioning, footwork, tool development and lots of sparring while wearing protective gear. As Bruce's TV work grew, Dan Inosanto took over the roll of sifu at the school. Bruce would call in from time to time to check on the progress although he continued to teach a small group of students privately at his home. Bruce would often use these times to experiment with the new techniques and themes on his students.

Around 1966/67 Bruce came up with the name 'Jeet Kune Do', which translates as 'Way of the Intercepting Fist', and the principle of interception was the defining characteristic that set it apart from other martial arts of the time and clearly showed the western fencing influence from his studies.

In December 1971 Bruce and his family moved back to Hong Kong to continue his development in the movie business. He closed down the Chinatown school and allowed Dan Inosanto to teach a small group of select students in his garage in Carson, California. When this group reached around a dozen students, they got together and built a gym in Dan's backyard.

Bruce Lee died suddenly on 20 July, 1973 of cerebral edoema; the reasons why he developed it were never pinned down. His death came as a great shock to the backyard students, especially to Dan Inosanto, who lost his sifu and was left feeling bereft and unsure what to do. With the encouragement of his students and friends he became convinced that he should preserve and perpetuate his sifu's teachings.

A year later, Dan Inosanto changed jobs and moved to Harbor City. The backyard was too small to accommodate all the equipment they had plus Bruce Lee's training apparatus, so a decision was made to open a school in partnership with Richard Bustillo. They opened the 'Filipino Kali Academy', teaching basic self-defence, boxing and Filipino martial arts. It also served as a place to perpetuate Bruce Lee's art of Jeet Kune Do.

Up to the point of his death Bruce was still exploring and growing, his art changing along the way to suit his personal needs. What is left now is a group of senior Bruce Lee students who teach what Bruce taught up to the time of his death. There is also a group that teach what Bruce Lee taught but have continued to evolve in their own personal direction. Above all, there remains Bruce Lee's philosophy, which can be used as a guide to inspire us to greater things in martial arts and in life: after all, Jeet Kune Do is known as a 'prescription for personal growth'.

Philosophy: 'Martial Arts For Life'

What is a martial artist? 'Martial' means warlike, the art of fighting. 'Art' is an imaginative, creative, human skill and an 'artist' is one who makes his craft a fine art. Collectively it seems, we have a person who is perfecting the art of fighting, so if martial arts in their original form were designed to take life, the above heading, 'Martial Arts for Life', seems to be a contradiction. However, this is not the case.

Why does one take up martial arts in the first place, spending so much time learning how to fight, investing countless years of training for a situation that may be over in just a few seconds? The obvious answer is self-preservation: those precious few seconds could be the difference between life and death. Although self-defence is the primary reason for studying martial arts, over the years deeper qualities are revealed. From the discipline of regular training comes an inner self-confidence, a belief in one's abilities and an ego that is in check. The positive qualities of martial arts seem limitless: power, grace, agility, strength, flexibility, patience, self-expression and an inner beauty. The list is endless.

Simple – Direct – Non-Classical

Simple – direct – non-classical are the three cornerstones of Jeet Kune Do that form the philosophical base on which the structures of the physical art stand.

Simple Keeping it simple allows us to apply a technique in the most efficient manner. If it takes four moves to defend against an attack, the Jeet Kune Do response would be 'Can I defend against it in three moves, or two moves, or even one move?' The fewer moves it takes, the higher the chance of success you will have against an uncooperative opponent.

Direct A technique can be simple but still not direct. A block, then punch or parry, then punch are surely simple, but a more efficient and direct way would be to simultaneously block a hit, or simply to intercept it with a hit of your own.

Non-classical This is related to the idea of directness in Jeet Kune Do. If someone grabs you there is no set pattern of response,

just a simple and direct hit. If someone takes your watch and then throws it at you, you catch it instantly. You do not drop into a classical stance or posture, then try to catch the watch – that would be too late.

In order to abide by the guiding philosophy of Jeet Kune Do – to be simple, direct and non-classical – one needs to hack away the unessential, be it the number of moves to get the job done or the economy of motion in a single move. To become 'non-telegraphic' is to hack away at the tell-tale signs of your motion. To be simple and direct takes years of training and refinement, and requires constant maintenance of the basic core structure.

The Three Stages of Cultivation

In the martial arts there are three stages of cultivation. These describe the journey of a martial artist.

Stage One The first stage is known as 'innocence' or 'original ignorance'. In self-defence one would react in any way possible to survive an attack. One has no idea of correct form or a set way to defend oneself, so a reaction would primarily be a primitive act of self-preservation.

Stage Two In the second stage one enters the world of martial arts. This stage is known as the stage of 'sophistication', the mechanical stage where you learn how to stand, punch and kick with economy of motion. You learn a scientific way of delivering the tools. The grooving of the neuro-muscular pathways takes years of training and thousands of repetitions of technique to have good structure and form. At this stage some of that 'original ignorance' is lost and one deals with all kinds of inner opposition and resistance: the mind can hesitate, or form an attachment to a technique where one can think too long about something and lose the natural flow of changing from movement to movement. This stage is also known as the 'abiding' stage. It becomes not only a physical game, but a mental one too.

Stage Three The third stage, or the 'spontaneous' stage, is the stage of 'letting go'. A state of mental clarity is developed. One no longer tries to be anything, one just 'is', like water, purposeless and formless; one flows, adapts and grows. In this state of 'no mind', one transcends the mechanical stage and becomes free. The art is internalized, one no longer thinks about the technique, it happens all by itself. No longer confined, one returns to that original state of ignorance/innocence, rediscovering that sense of freedom. With the senses completely awakened you are in a flowing process, able to fit in with an opponent and adapting to the ever-changing flow of combat. There is no confining centre and no limitation – without the mental chatter, one is simply 'in the moment'.

The Water Principles

In the nature of water we find the guiding principle of Jeet Kune Do. Like water, one should be in a continuous state of flow. Water has no shape or form, so it can become all forms; it is the softest substance that penetrates the hardest. Water can crash, destroying everything in its path; it can adapt and change its course without thought, or seep through the tiniest crack. To flow like water in the face of adversity is to experience the freedom to adapt spontaneously to whatever circumstance may face you in combat and in life.

Learning how to fight, then being able to fight, somehow creates a state of being that lessens the need for ever having to actually fight. In learning to fight an opponent, one has faced that inner fear and gone beyond into a realm where you come to understand more about yourself. It is no longer just an arena in which to fight an opponent, it becomes an arena to watch how one's mind works. 'Martial arts' takes on an added meaning as a vehicle to a deeper understanding of one's true nature. It becomes an investigation of freedom, not only in fighting but in life. Essentially, the martial arts become a vehicle of self-expression; it becomes an intensified awareness of flow in movement and this movement is an expression of that life.

One comes to realise that the pursuit of this creativity in martial arts goes way beyond a few hours' training a week; it becomes an integral part of one's daily existence. Martial art is like cultivating a small area of a field. The real challenge is to be completely awake 'in the moment' of every day, allowing the skills developed in training to spill over and nourish the whole field of our existence, enhancing that quality of our life and that of others.

In the context of martial arts, art is much more than just a skill. The aesthetic of martial art is a feeling of life, when in those rare moment we become one with nature and experience a knowledge through the senses from which skills and awareness are at work artistically.

So you see, indeed, martial arts are for life.

Fig 2. The author, Dave Carnell.

2 The Bai-Jong or On-Guard Position

The Bai-Jong or On-Guard position is the key to Jeet Kune Do's success. It is the platform from which all attack and defence comes. Its structure allows for simultaneous attack and defence, explosive footwork and dynamic trapping hands.

At a casual glance the on-guard position looks pretty much like any other boxing or kickboxing stance: one leg in front with both hands held up protecting the face. In fact this is the definition given by many instructors. So what makes it uniquely Jeet Kune Do? To find out we need to break down the structure of the stance into its various components.

Foot Positioning

Draw a straight line on the floor. Place the front (lead) foot's big toe on the line and the rear foot's heel on the line. Turn the feet to approximately 45 degrees. The length of the base, that is the distance between the feet, varies depending on the length of the legs – a long-legged person will have a longer base. The base is generally longer than a normal walking step forward. It is more like a stride (see Figs 3–4).

Fig 3. Right lead on-guard, toe in line with rear heel.

Fig 4. Side on-guard, toe in line with rear heel.

Fig 5. Raised rear heel.

Fig 6. Rear tail.

Rear Heel

The rear heel is raised slightly off the floor, which is the key to the explosiveness of the stance. It is not just raised, it is spring loaded. By lowering the centre of gravity more load is placed onto the rear leg. This is like compressing a coiled spring ready to shoot you forward when you let go (see Fig 5).

The Tail Principle

The tail refers to the measure between the rear knee and the rear heel, that is, the part of the leg that sticks out behind the trunk of the body. Maximizing the length of the tail will enable greater potential for exploding forward. Draw a straight line down from the rear shoulder to the rear knee (see Fig 6).

This will give you the perfect guide line for your own individual body frame. The edge of the knee should just touch this line. To maximize the tail just lower the centre of gravity a little, and you will find the rear knee moves in front of the line. Move the rear foot back a little to realign the knee on the line. This will give you greater potential to explode forward. If the knee moves too far away from this line you may find that you have greater stability but lose the ability to explode forward. There is a fine line between having stability and an explosive stance. You have to play with it.

The hips and shoulders turn in to face the same direction as the feet, making the body a smaller target. Knees should be slightly bent,

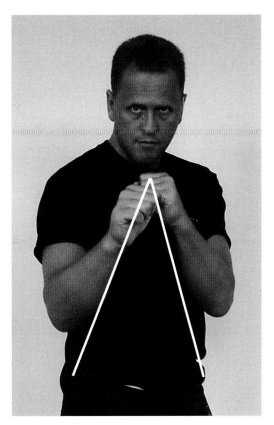

Fig 7. Front view of the wedge.

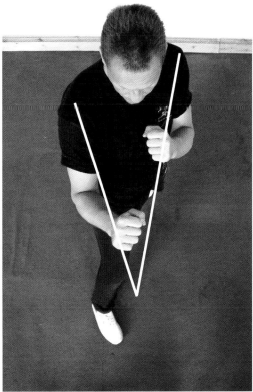

Fig 8. The wedge from above.

never locked. The head faces forward with chin lowered slightly and shoulders are raised and rolled forward to protect the face.

The Wedge Principle

This is the key to the upper body's simultaneous attack and defence. If you draw two imaginary lines from the hips to the opponent's chin in front of you, you will create a wedge shape. This forms the lines on which to rest the forearms, with both hands protecting the centre line (see Figs 7–9).

The maximum distance of the lead elbow from the lead hip is measured by stretching the thumb and little finger of the opposite hand out, crossing in front of the body and placing the thumb on the front hip with the

Fig 9. Side view of the wedge.

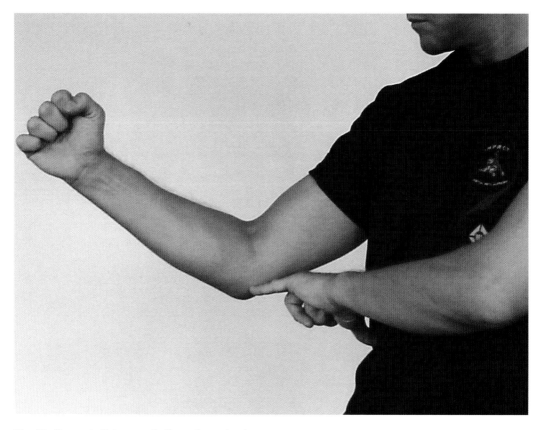

Fig 10. Correct distance of elbow from body.

elbow touching the tip of the little finger while resting on the wedge line referred to as the runway. The lead hand can move freely along this line so long as it doesn't move beyond the thumb and little finger measure (see Fig 10).

All of the above key points combine together to give a stance or platform from which to attack, defend and counter-attack. The stance is strong and firm but at the same time allows movement in all directions, especially exploding forwards.

3 Footwork

In Jeet Kune Do, footwork is about purposeful movement. It is no good bouncing around using up energy. The body should be in a continual state of alertness, ready to move at a moment's notice – imagine an on-board motor constantly ticking over ready to move in any direction at a split second's notice. Footwork is a relationship with an opponent, it should be practised until it is natural and instinctive.

The key to superior footwork is to have total command of the on-guard stance, paying particular attention to the rear heel and rear leg tail. Whether you move your front foot two inches or lunge forward several feet, it is all considered 'footwork'. Once you are moving, it is easy enough to gather speed; what is more important is being able to move quickly off the mark and generating enough force to explode forward.

Distance and the Fighting Measure

The distance between two opponents is referred to as the fighting measure. Whoever controls this distance usually controls the fight.

It is essential that you develop a feel for your own fighting measure. The length of your own tools and the speed with which they are delivered are important factors in deciding the optimal distance. The speed and ability of an opponent must also be taken into account, hence the relationship.

The ideal distance is referred to as 'standing on the brim of fire'. This is the distance where an opponent cannot reach you with a simple attack without the preparation of a step.

Of course, in sparring both fighters will be making small movements to try to make their opponent make errors in judgement of distance, bringing them off balance or open for counter-attack.

In Jeet Kune Do, footwork is kept very simple. There are four basic types of footwork: advance, retreat, side step right and side step left.

The Shuffle or Step and Slide

The shuffle, or step and slide, advance and retreat is used to maintain the fighting measure. This is what keeps you out of an opponent's range and just outside of your hitting range. The shuffle is used to constantly feel for the right distance to set up a position for an explosive attack, or to make an opponent over-reach, thus setting up an interceptive attack.

When advancing, take a small step forward with the lead foot then slide up the rear foot the same distance to maintain the on-guard position (see Figs 11–13). When retreating, take a small step back with the rear foot, maintaining the raised rear heel, then slide the front foot back the same distance (see Figs 14–16). A key point when advancing is not to lift the foot up too high from the ground when stepping forward as this will 'telegraph' the advancing forward motion to the opponent. It should feel almost as though it is the front leg shin that moves the foot forward.

Fig 11. Bai-jong on-guard.

Fig 14. Bai-jong on-guard.

Fig 12. Lead step.

Fig 13. Slide up the rear foot into bai-jong.

Fig 15. Step back with the rear foot.

Fig 16. Slide lead foot back to on-guard.

The Push-Shuffle

The push-shuffle advance is the explosive lunge forward off the ball of the foot of the rear leg. It is a key part of Jeet Kune Do's attack, bridging the gap between you and an opponent in one explosive lunge forward, catching him by surprise.

Using the coiled spring effect of the rear heel, push forward off the back foot, stepping out with the front foot to cover some distance. Then slide the rear foot up to regain the on-guard position (see Figs 17–19).

To retreat with the push-shuffle, load the front leg (that is, transfer weight onto the front leg) and push backwards as the rear foot steps back. Then slide the front foot back to regain the on-guard position (see Figs 20–22).

Fig 17. On-guard position.

Fig 20. On-guard.

Fig 18. Push-shuffle forward.

Fig 19. To on-guard.

Fig 21. Push-shuffle back.

Fig 22. To on-guard.

Slide Step

From the on-guard position, slide the back foot up to the front foot then step forward with the lead foot. Resume the on-guard position. This movement should be done quickly so that you are not caught with both feet together (see Figs 23–25).

In reverse, slide the lead foot back, then step back with the rear foot and recover the on-guard position quickly.

In advance, the slide step enables you to cover the ground more quickly. In retreat it allows you to avoid being hit, for example, if you need to retreat to avoid an opponent's side kick (see Figs 26–27).

Fig 23. On-guard.

Fig 24. Slide up rear foot.

Fig 25. Step forward with lead foot.

Fig 26. On-guard facing an opponent.

Fig 27. A slide step retreat evades a side kick.

The Pendulum

This is a variation of the slide step. The footwork remains the same and the trunk of the body remains almost in the same place (see Figs 28–30).

The pendulum can be used to avoid lowline kicks or to set up a probe with your own lead kick (see Figs 31–32 and 33–35).

Fig 28. On-guard.

Fig 29. Pendulum forward.

Fig 30. Pendulum back.

Fig 31. On-guard facing an opponent.

Fig 32. Pendulum back to avoid low-line attack.

Fig 33. On-guard facing an opponent.

Fig 34. Lead hook kick as a probe.

Fig 35. Pendulum retreat.

Fig 36. On-guard.

Fig 37. Lead step.

Fig 40. On-guard.

Fig 41. Lead foot steps back.

The Step Slide Step

This is an example of how to combine various footwork patterns. Here the combination of the step slide (shuffle) and the slide step enables a greater distance to be covered.

Take a small step with the lead foot, now slide the rear foot up to the lead then step out with the lead foot (see Figs 36–39).

In advance, this footwork can allow you to set up a lead leg kick from a greater distance. In retreat, it can help you to clear more distance if you feel you are being pressured by an opponent (see Figs 40–43).

Fig 38. Slide rear leg up.

Fig 39. Step forward with lead foot to on-guard.

Fig 42. Slide lead foot back.

Fig 43. Rear foot steps back to on-guard.

The Lateral Step

Moving right and left is accomplished by lateral steps. If you are in a right lead on-guard stance and want to move to the right then move the right foot to the side, followed by the left foot moving to the right. Make the steps small so you do not leave the groin open to attack (see Figs 44–46). Similarly, if you want to move to the left from a right on-guard stance, take a step to the left with the left foot followed by a step to the left with the right lead foot (see Figs 47–49). A simple key is to move the foot that is the closest to the direction in which you want to move first, being careful not to cross the feet and maintaining the on-guard position at all times.

Fig 44. On-guard facing forward.

Fig 47. On-guard.

Fig 45. Right foot takes a small step to the right.

Fig 46. Left foot slides across to on-guard.

Fig 48. Rear foot steps to the left.

Fig 49. Lead foot slides across to on-guard.

The Curve Step

The curve step is similar to the lateral step but positions the body at an angle towards an opponent. If you are in a right on-guard stance take a step to the right with the right foot, then, using the right foot as a pivot, swing the left foot out, re-positioning at an angle to your opponent (see Figs 50–55).

Fig 50. On-guard.

Fig 53. On-guard.

Fig 51. Right foot steps to the side.

Fig 52. Pivot on lead foot swinging rear leg out.

Fig 54. Rear foot steps to the side.

Fig 55. Pivot on rear foot, sliding lead leg over.

Fig 56. On-guard facing an opponent.

To move to the left from a right on-guard position, simply move the left foot to the left, using it as a pivot when repositioning the right foot slightly to the left (see Figs 53–55). This is sometimes used in countering an opponent's attempt to trap your lead hand (see Figs 56–58).

Exercises to Improve Footwork

- Using a skipping rope teaches you to be able to handle your own body weight and keeps you on the balls of your feet.
- Running, as well as being a great cardio-vascular workout, strengthens the legs, giving you more energy.
- Medium squatting and lunging motions increase leg strength and control.
- Leg stretching will allow you to get off the mark faster without injury.

- Shadow sparring is good practice for putting footwork together with various tools.
- Actual sparring with an equally mobile opponent improves both timing and distance control.

A good exercise is the 'mirror drill'. This helps develop a natural aliveness with footwork and helps with control of maintaining distance. Face off with an opponent at a distance where you can only just reach with a rear thrust kick (standing on the brim of fire). Have the opponent use any of the footwork patterns used in Jeet Kune Do. If he advances you retreat, if he retreats you advance. Similarly, if the opponent side steps left you side step right and if he side steps right you side step left, so maintaining the fighting measure. Then reverse the drill so that you become the director.

Finally, the best exercise for footwork is to do more footwork!

Fig 57. Opponent steps in to trap and hit.

Fig 58. Step and pivot as you counter-trap and hit.

4 Defence

In Jeet Kune Do the priority lies in attack, the principle being 'offence is the best form of defence'. Not letting an opponent's attack get started and keeping him continually on the defence relies on a strong aggressive attack, taking control of the fight away from an opponent. Sometimes it takes the form of a timed hit or hitting into an opponent's hit, which can neutralize his attack.

Sometimes, however, command of the fight may be lost and when this happens you are put on the defensive. This can happen for various reasons. The opponent may be faster or stronger, you might get caught up in a flurry of punches forcing you on the defence, you may get taken by a surprise attack or tagged with a really good shot.

'Defence' comprises any measures you take to off-set an attack to prevent it from landing on its intended target. In Jeet Kune Do there are many forms of defence:

- Distance/footwork
- Evasiveness
- Parry and hit (four-corner defence)
- Block/cover and hit
- Interception/timed hits

Distance/Footwork

The primary aim of Jeet Kune Do is to hit an opponent without being hit yourself. This is difficult but becomes a little easier if you are very mobile and able to move in all directions quickly without much preparation.

This is one of the reasons why the bai-jong on-guard stance is of great importance to the Jeet Kune Do practitioner. The bai-jong is designed to be firm but highly mobile, allowing for freedom of movement.

In defence, footwork can make an opponent's tools miss their target. It is also a way for you to conserve energy. By retreating or side stepping, you can bring an opponent off balance, leaving him open for a counter-attack. As you gain and break ground you can make him misjudge his own distance causing him to over-commit his attack and bring himself off balance. At this moment you will catch him at the point of helplessness (see Figs 59–61).

Fig 59. On-guard facing an opponent.

Evasiveness

Evasiveness is the realm of the counter-fighter. Holding ground and moving the head or trunk just enough will make an opponent's blow miss its target. Evading leaves both hands free to counter. In Jeet Kune Do it is important to have an aggressive defence, that is, you should aim to hit simultaneously as you evade or immediately follow an evasive move with a hit.

Slipping

Slipping is used against straight line punches to the head from an opponent's lead or rear hand. It involves shifting the head to either side of the punch by rolling the shoulders.

Slipping an opponent's right jab while in right on-guard stance As an opponent feeds a right lead jab, roll your right shoulder forward and down. Your head will shift off the line of attack and his punch will travel

over your shoulder. Economy of motion is important: you move just enough to make him miss. Sometimes it will feel as if their fist or forearm just skims the side of your ear. That is how close it should be (see Fig 62).

Fig 62. Slipping the jab.

Fig 60. Evade using footwork.

Fig 61. Bringing an opponent off balance to strike.

39

Fig 63. Slipping the left jab.

Fig 64. Slipping the left rear straight.

Slipping an opponent's left jab while in right on-guard stance As an opponent feeds a left jab, roll your left shoulder forward and down, shifting your head off the line of attack (see Fig 63).

Slipping an opponent's left rear straight while in right on-guard stance As an opponent feeds a left rear straight, roll your left shoulder forward and down, shifting your head off the line of attack (see Fig 64).

Slipping an opponent's right rear straight while in right on-guard stance As an opponent feeds a right rear straight, roll your right shoulder forward and down, slightly shifting your head off the line of attack (see Fig 65).

Fig 65. Slipping the right rear straight.

Fig 66. Slip and simultaneously hit against the right jab.

Fig 67. Slip and simultaneously hit against the left rear straight.

Once you have mastered the slip it is time to put in either simultaneous hits, or slip first then hit (see Figs 66–67).

The Bob

The bob is similar to the slip in that you move to the outside or inside of the punch. Bending forward at the waist enables you to counter with body shots. Bending your knees also drops you lower than the slip and is a good way to set up take-downs by moving into grappling (see Figs 68–70).

Fig 68. Bob and hit against the jab.

Fig 69. Bob and hit against the right rear straight.

Fig 70. Bob to set up a take-down.

Fig 71. On-guard facing forward.

Fig 72. Bob to the right.

Fig 73. Weave.

The Bob and Weave

The bob and weave is used against heavy hooking blows or swings. By bobbing inside the lead or rear hook you pull yourself inside the line of an opponent's attack, then weave underneath his punch, so it travels over your head. Counter hits can take place as you weave with a body hook or as you come out of the weave with a follow-up shot (see Figs 71–79).

Fig 74. Come up on the left side.

Fig 75. Back to on-guard.

Fig 76. Bob to the left.

Fig 77. Weave.

Fig 78. Come up on the right.

Fig 79. Back to on-guard.

Fig 80. On-guard facing an opponent.

Fig 81. Opponent starts to feed a lead hook, bob inside.

Fig 82. Weave under and lead body hook.

Fig 83. To rear cross.

Great care is needed when using the bob and weave as it can leave you open to an opponent's knee strikes or uppercuts. When you bend forward with the bob keep your hands in front of your face. Use this move sparingly (see Figs 80–87).

Fig 84. On-guard facing an opponent.

Fig 85. Opponent fires a rear hook, you bob inside.

Fig 86. Weave under with a rear body hook.

Fig 87. Follow with a lead hook.

Fig 88. Facing an opponent in bai-jong.

Fig 89. Counter the jab with the snap-back.

The Snap Back

The snap back is a fast, defensive pull back against the jab. The movement of the trunk pulls the chin away from an opponent's lead jab. When snapping your head and trunk back, lower your rear heel slightly, maintaining the spring-load effect. Take care not to touch the ground or you will make it difficult to spring back with a counter-strike. (see Figs 88–89).

The Shoulder Roll

This is a defence against the rear straight. As an opponent feeds a rear punch, roll your front shoulder up and away, transferring your weight on to the back foot. This is a similar motion to throwing a lead hook punch. Your chin should be tucked inside the lead shoulder with the rear hand helping to cover the face. Make sure that you do not look away to the side – you need to keep looking forward to see what is happening at all times. As an opponent's rear cross returns back to its starting position, be prepared to counter-attack with your own rear straight or lead back fist. It is also possible to counter during the shoulder roll motion with a lead kick of your own (see Figs 90–91).

Fig 90. Facing an opponent in on-guard.

Fig 91. Opponent feeds a rear straight counter with a shoulder roll.

Fig 92. Facing an opponent in bai-jong.

Fig 93. As opponent jabs, duck and jab.

The Duck

As an opponent feeds a lead jab, simply bend the knees and drop down, keeping the hands in front of the face and letting his punch go over your head. This will allow you to hit their body with either hand (see Figs 92–93).

Parry and Hit

The parry is used to deflect a blow off the intended line of attack and is usually done with a cupped hand. This will leave them open for counter attack. It is important not to overreach with the parry as this will lead to an opponent changing the line of attack during the middle of your move. Parry at the last possible moment and always be ready to counter-attack. Parries should be backed up with body evasion and footwork, allowing you to parry and hit simultaneously.

The art of parrying and hitting simultaneously is known as lin sil die dar, and is a faster method of defence than parrying first and then hitting. It has its roots in the Wing Chun system of gung fu but has been somewhat modified for the Jeet Kune Do structure known as the 'four corners' simultaneous attack and defence.

The Four Corners

The structure of Jeet Kune Do's defence is based on that of an imaginary window frame, divided in half by a centre line which runs down the centre of the body, then divided again by three horizontal lines across the body: one line across the eyebrows, the second across the solar plexus and the third across the groin. Two vertical lines running down both sides of the shoulders form the outer boundaries of the frame. This structure forms four distinct areas known as the 'four corners'. The area inside this frame is known as your 'airspace' and if anything enters these four areas you have to deal with it. Keeping your defensive parries within these boundaries is the art of good defence (see Fig 94). It is possible to defend the four corners with both the lead and

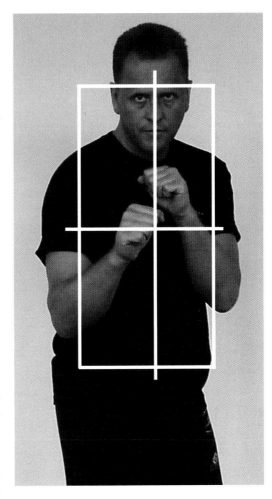

Fig 94. The four corners.

Fig 95. Side view bai-jong.

Fig 96. Biu-san chung-chuie.

Fig 97. Ha-pak chung-chuie.

Fig 98. Loy-ha-pak chung-chuie.

rear hand, although Jeet Kune Do tends to prefer rear hand parries, allowing you to hit simultaneously with the lead hand.

If you take a right bai-jong ready position (see Fig 95) the left upper corner is covered with a biu-sau outer forearm cover (see Fig 96). The right upper corner is covered with woang-pak, the high cross parry (see Fig 97). The lower corner is covered by loy-ha-pak, a sweeping semi-circular parry which clears that area (see Fig 98). The lower right corner is covered with ouy-ha-pak, a low slapping parry which clears this side (see Fig 99).

It is important to practice economy of

Fig 99. Ouy-ha-pak chung-chuie.

Fig 100. Biu-san chung-chuie.

Fig 101. Ouy-ha-pak chung-chuie.

Fig 102. Loy-ha-pak chung-chuie.

Fig 103. High ha-pak chung-chuie.

movement when using the corner parries and to keep within the boundaries. Over-parrying will open up another line of attack for your opponent. Combining the four corner defence with evasion skills will make you a smaller target by reducing the defensive airspace. Most parrying is made safer by angling the body. Slipping the head and adding footwork puts you in a more advantageous position to return the attack (see Figs 100–103).

Block Cover and Hit

Blocking, or covering, is probably the easiest form of defence yet the least desirable, as it can sometimes leave you off balance and out of position to counter. The idea is to create a defensive shield or shell around the head and body using the arms to cover an opponent's line of attack. The legs can also be used to shield attacks below the waist. To defend hooking punches to the head simply collapse the forearm to the biceps and place the hand over the ear to make a defensive shield. At the same time lower the centre of gravity and bend your knees slightly to absorb the force of the blow. This will help to keep you on balance. Be ready to counter-strike (see Figs 104–105).

Hooks to the body are covered in a similar way. By pulling the elbows back and down into the side of the body and raising the hip slightly at the same time, you can make a defensive wall. The biceps and forearm will absorb the force into the compact arm (see Figs 106–107).

Fig 104. Forearm cover against a lead hook.

Fig 105. Forearm cover against a rear hook.

Fig 106. Elbow cover against a rear body hook.

Fig 107. Elbow cover against a lead body hook.

Fig 108. Rear elbow tuck against a lead jab to body.

Fig 109. Lead elbow tuck against a rear straight to body.

Jabs and rear straights to the body can be picked up with either forearm pulling in across the centre line (see Figs 108–109).

Defending kicks below the waist can be dealt with by using good footwork. If you have a good command of the fighting measure you can intercept with a kick of your own, but more often than not the low kick is thrown in the midst of a combination and there is no time to move the intended target out of the way. Here, a leg shield is needed to solve the problem. This involves raising the knee and placing the lower leg in the line of attack, creating a defensive shield (see Fig 110).

To defend against a rear oblique kick, snap the calf back towards your thigh, often striking an opponent's inside calf muscle with the point of the knee (see Fig 111).

In Jeet Kune Do we strive for non-passive movement, hitting on the opponent's intention to attack. This does not mean you can never use a passive defence, it just means try to avoid passive, defensive moves. If footwork is used to defend against an opponent's attack, it should be to bring him off balance or to set up a counter-attack. If body evasion is used, try to hit at the same time or, put the body in a position where you can hit an opponent but where it is hard for him to hit you without repositioning. It is important to have command of all defensive methods, even though some are more efficient than others. Sometimes it may be more effective to block or cover – it all comes down to control of the fighting measure and the relationship with the opponent.

Fig 110. Leg shield against a rear round kick.

Fig 111. Pulling the calf back against an oblique kick.

5 Tools of the Trade

The Lead Straight

The lead straight punch is a core offensive technique in Jeet Kune Do. It is often used as the tool to intercept an opponent's attack. It is simple and direct, travelling the shortest distance between two points. It also gives you a powerful tool in the front line of fire.

Standing strong side forward brings the hand closer to the desired target. Because the lead hand has less distance to travel, a unique method of conveying force into the punch has been developed. From a stationary bai-jong, the delivery starts in the rear foot with the heel pivoting inwards to relay the force through the hips, shoulder, elbow and out through the fist. In order to make the punch non-telegraphic, there should be no retraction of the hand before it fires (see Figs 112–113).

In advancing, the lead hand moves first and everything else follows, which adds economy of motion to the structure of the punch. By pushing off with the rear foot (push-shuffle) you take up power from the ground relaying the moving weight into a small impact area of the bottom three knuckles of the vertical fist.

This is accomplished by use of a 'falling step', or 'drop step', as I like to call it. It is a unique way of training body weight transfer into the punch. As you step forward with the lead foot, let the body fall forward, using the pull of gravity, hitting the target before the front foot is grounded. The lead foot should not land before the fist makes contact or the body weight will transfer back into the ground instead of behind the punch (see Figs 114–116).

Fig 112. On-guard facing an opponent.

Fig 113. Stationary lead straight.

Fig 114. On-guard facing an opponent.

Fig 117. Lead straight showing the power line.

Fig 115. Lead hand moves first.

Fig 116. Push-shuffle lead straight.

The fist is held in the vertical position to maximize the impact of the strike along the power line, a line which runs all the way from the shoulder down the arm and out through the first knuckle from the bottom. Keeping the elbow down allows for complete transfer of body weight into the fist, the arms being merely part of the whole body unity. Remember to hit with the whole body, not just the arms. Having the elbow down also means there is less recoil and more force relayed into the target (see Fig 117). The key to the lead straight is the synchronization of its various components.

Stage 1 Take up the bai-jong on-guard position. The lead arm from the elbow to the hand will be resting along the imaginary line running from the lead hip to the opponent's chin. This is referred to as the 'runway'. In slow motion, move the lead hand forward along the runway then quickly push off from the ball of the foot of the rear leg as you complete the arm extension. This is in keeping with the principle of 'hand moves before the foot'.

Stage 2 From an on-guard bai-jong position, take a long, quick step forward with the lead

Fig 118. Raise lead leg in foot obstruct position.

foot. This will trigger the forward spring of the rear leg from the ball of the foot. Taking up power from the ground, explode forward.

Stage 3 This involves the use of the focus glove. From the on-guard position raise the lead leg into a leg obstruction position. The foot will be raised at knee height. Allow the leg to drop down whilst pushing off the rear leg. Make contact with the focus pad before the lead foot touches the ground. This develops depth of penetration with full body weight behind the punch (see Figs 118–119).

Stage 4 Return to bai-jong or use the lead straight together with other tools, for example:
• Lead hook kick to groin to lead straight
• Lead straight to lead hook kick
• Lead straight as a timed hit against an opponent's punch
• Lead straight in conjunction with hand immobilization

Fig 119. Drop-step forward lead straight.

- Lead straight in the midst of a punching combination
- Lead straight to a straight blast
- Leg obstruction to a lead straight
- Stop-kick to lead straight.

To get a good idea of the force generating the power of the lead straight imagine this. Take a 45lb barbell and attach it to a chain hanging from the ceiling with one end of the barbell facing your opponent, then swing it at your opponent. This is now 45lb in motion, and when you focus that weight into a small area, like the tip of the barbell or the bottom three knuckles of your hand, the effect is devastating.

Although the lead straight can be developed into a highly destructive blow it should not be an end in itself. It is a means to an end and should be reinforced and supported with other tools.

The Straight Blast: Jik-Chung-Chuie

The straight blast is a simple offensive form of attack. It is easy to develop and combines well with other techniques to culminate in an attack that is hard to defend against.

Its origin lies in the Wing Chun system of gung fu. The essence of the technique is its piston-like repetitive punching down the centre line. The barrage of punches overwhelms the opponent, keeping him off balance and making it hard for him to cover.

Jeet Kune Do's version of this punch remains essentially the same as the Wing Chun straight blast, but it has a modified delivery system, giving it a flavour of its own.

Both arms fire along the offensive/defensive wedge structure that is built into the bai-jong on-guard frame. Whilst one arm fires forward, the other arm is chambering ready

to fire. Each consecutive punch follows on from the next in rapid succession. The fists travel side by side as each arm pumps out along the runway created by the wedge formation. The forearms form a deflective shield, cutting into an opponent's attack and giving you centre line advantage as your footwork explodes you forward. It is important to keep constant forward pressure in your technique but not so much that if the opponent were to side step you would fall forward on your face (see Figs 120–124).

The vertical fist alignment of the arm allows for the 'power line' to come into play. The power line is the imaginary line that runs down the arm from the shoulder exiting through the second knuckle up from the little finger. Punching along this power line brings about a three-knuckle strike so that no one knuckle takes the full force of the blow. This helps to protect the hand. Turning the fist in

Fig 120. On-guard facing forward.

Fig 121. Straight blast rear chung-chuie moves forward.

Fig 122. Full extension of rear punch.

Fig 125. On-guard facing an opponent.

Fig 126. Jik-chung-chuie.

Fig 127. To right punch.

slightly gives the best alignment of the bone structure in the arms, relaying more force into the opponent with less reverberation back into the shoulder (see Figs 125–127).

The key to a good, effective straight blast is timing and distance. It normally follows some kind of entry or interception of the opponent's attack. If you start your straight blast too far away you will lose the element of surprise. If you are too close you will lose power and jam up your own technique. If the timing is right, the forward pressure of the technique will have an opponent moving backwards, breaking his base and destroying his structure.

Fig 123. Rear chung-chuie travels back as lead chung-chuie moves forward.

Fig 124. Lead chung-chuie at full extension.

Although the jik-chung-chuie straight blast is an integral part of Jeet Kune Do's fighting method, it should be used sparingly. At the right time it will always have that element of surprise. Catching an opponent with the onslaught of the blast when he is least prepared is sometimes all it takes to overpower him.

Exercises for the Straight Blast

Have a training partner hold two focus pads against his shoulder. Concentrate on punching with full power, snapping through the pad with a 2in (5cm) penetration.

Once this feels comfortable, have the pad man retreat as you straight blast with advancing footwork. Make sure your punches go forward and through the target. Do not fall into the habit of circling your punches as though you were hammering down, as this will cause you to scrape down the focus pads instead of penetrating through.

The pad man, while retreating, can also slow down or speed up or even hold his ground. This will force you to develop a better feel for the punch under different degrees of pressure or resistance (see Figs 128–130). Try straight blasting in the air whilst holding small hand weights. This gets the elbows used to the lockout snap that is needed for the explosive

Fig 128. Straight blast on focus pads.

Fig 129. Right lead.

Fig 130. To rear chung-chuie.

Fig 131. On-guard with hand weights.

Fig 132. Straight blast.

Fig 133. Punching along the wedge.

power of the chung-chuie. Then try to create the same feeling of heaviness in the punch without the weights, like being hit with an iron ball on the end of a chain (see Figs 131–133.)

The Finger Jab: Biu-Jee

The lead finger jab is the longest hand weapon in Jeet Kune Do. Its primary target is the eyes, which are extremely sensitive to even the slightest touch. It is almost impossible to stop the uncontrollable watering of the eyes when a foreign object enters them. We have all experienced the feeling of a 'fly in the eye', when all systems stop while we try to remove the object.

Little force is needed to use the finger jab. It does not rely on power, as speed and accuracy are the keys. It should feel like a snap rather than a push. The finger jab can be used to disrupt, temporarily blind or confuse and demoralize an aggressive opponent.

The mechanics of the biu-jee are the same as a lead straight. The lead forearm rests along the runway (lead side of the wedge) and the arm is snapped out loosely to the target. It is important to align the tips of the index, middle and fourth fingers by bending the middle finger slightly. This gives you the correct hand formation so that no damage to the fingers takes place should you be slightly off target and strike a bony area (see Figs 134–135).

At long range, the finger jab can be thrown from different angles. If you are in a right lead bai-jong you can lower the lead hand so that it is close to the front of the lead thigh, then fire the biu-jee vertically towards the target. This angle is hard for the opponent to pick up and is often felt before it is seen (see Figs 136–137).

Another option is to position the right hand low on the left side of the wedge so

Fig 134. On-guard.

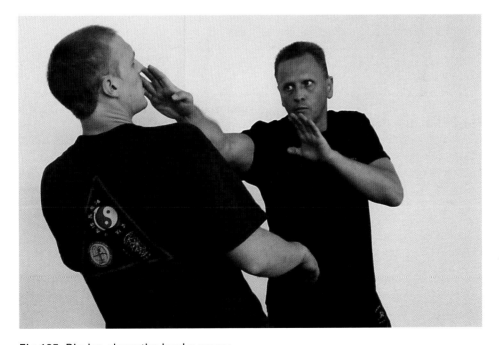

Fig 135. Biu-jee along the lead runway.

Fig 136. From long range lead hand on lead thigh.

Fig 137. Biu-jee finger jab.

that you appear to be in a shoulder roll position, then fire the biu-jee along the left runway (see Figs 138–139).

The finger jab can also help to disguise footwork as you close the gap between yourself and your opponent. It is also a good way of pulling the body forward to generate explosive energy for kicks (see Figs 140–142).

The finger jab is obviously not a tool for the tournament competitor or general sparring situations. However, in a life-threatening situation this is one tool you do not want to be without.

Fig 138. Lead hand guard held on left runway.

Fig 139. Biu-jee thrown on an angle from the left side.

Fig 140. On-guard facing an opponent. Fig 141. Biu-jee disguises rear foot slide.

Fig 142. To side kick.

Fig 143. X-ray target.

Fig 144. Biu-jee finger jab.

Exercises for the Finger Jab

Unsurprisingly, it is difficult to find training partners who are willing to allow you to practise the finger jab on them, and you will only get so far practising in the air, hence the importance of good training equipment. Try hanging a tennis ball on a string from the ceiling and practising the finger jab from a variety of angles. As you become more proficient and accurate, increase the distance away from the ball and incorporate footwork at the same time. Another method is to suspend a piece of paper or x-ray film in the air and draw some half-inch diameter (1.2cm) circles on it. This will help you acquire accuracy as you pop the film with the quick snap of the finger jab. The motion should be whip-like as you retract the arm back to its ready position (see Figs 143–144).

The Jeet Kune Do Long Hook

The long hook deviates from the runway structure of the bai-jong by adding a long curved strike to your arsenal of attack.

It is used to break down an opponent's defensive cover, breaking his structure and leaving him open to attack (see Figs 145–147).

The long hook is a good tool when used in combination with the straight blast. Often an

Fig 145. Bird's-eye view of unmatched leads with focus gloves.

Fig 146. Lead hand curves off the runway.

Fig 147. Crashing through an opponent's lead arm.

Fig 148. On-guard, unmatched leads.

Fig 149. Rear chung-chuie is covered by an opponent.

opponent will raise his arm to cover up against the straight blast, and the long hook can then be used to clear his arms away, breaking his structure and bringing him off balance for further attack (see Figs 148–151).

The Jeet Kune Do Long Shovel

Like the long hook, the long shovel change angle of the lead hand attack along the rur making contact with the fist in a palm-up posr The striking areas are usually the solar plexu the chin. Again, this works well with the str blast (see Figs 152–153).

Fig 150. Long hook crashes through an opponent's guard.

Fig 151. Opening up a line for the rear chung-chuie.

Fig 152. Rear chung-chuie scores.

Fig 153. Opening up a line for the long shovel.

6   Kicks

In Jeet Kune Do the majority of the kicks are below the waist, in accordance with the principle of 'longest weapon to the closest target' – for example, the lead low side kick to the knee or shin of the opponent, or a lead hook kick to the groin. The principle of 'longest to the closest' helps with recovery back to the bai-jong on-guard stance. As the leg travels a shorter distance it takes less time to score. Care must be taken to maintain the integrity of the bai-jong, therefore the kicks that are chosen are the ones that least deviate from this position. The more direct the kicks are, the more chance they have of not being seen by the opponent, just felt.

A way to develop this economy of motion is to apply the wedge principle to your feet. Take a right lead on-guard stance, the front big toe in line with the rear heel, then draw two straight lines from the feet to the target. You will see the wedge shape. These two lines give the guiding runways for your kicks. If the feet deviate from these lines it will result in a less economical kick that can be telegraphed to the opponent (see Fig 154).

Fig 154. The kicking runway.

The Lead Stationary Hook Kick

The hook kick travels on the lead kicking runway by moving the lead foot first from a stationary position. Keeping the foot on the runway will mean that the knee will pass through the centre line (see Fig 155). At this point, the rear foot will pivot to face behind you which allows for the hips to be driven into the kick for added power.

The power comes from the pivot of the rear foot with the torquing of the hips. The contact area of the foot on impact is the

Fig 155. The lead knee passes through the centre line.

instep. If you are wearing a good shoe, the impact area can be the point of the toes or tip of the shoe. A good target area for the hook kick is the groin, or, if you have the flexibility, the hook kick can also reach up to the head (see Figs 156–158).

Exercises for the Hook Kick

Have your partner hold a focus pad at groin height and stand at a distance where you can reach the focus pad with the lead hook kick without taking a step. From the on-guard stance, raise the lead foot on the kicking runway. Practise the last part of the kick to help the co-ordination of the foot pivot, hip twist and snap of the kick. This drill will also improve balance as you continually stand on one foot.

Fig 156. On-guard facing an opponent.

Fig 157. Slide the rear leg up.

Fig 158. Lead hook to the groin.

Fig 159. On-guard.

Fig 160. Lead leg side kick.

The Stationary Side Kick

The target area for the side kick is the opponent's mid-section or his lead knee. As with the hook kick, the side kick travels out along the kicking runway. First the kicking foot moves, then the rear foot pivots, which turns the hip in and over, with the upper body tilting back to a 45-degree angle to avoid possible punches from the opponent. At the point of contact the shoulders should be aligned with the hip and knee. The contact area of the foot is the heel. This will give you a power line running up through the leg. When the kick is delivered, you should feel like you have stomped the target with your heel. It is important that once you have made contact and the foot has penetrated the target, you retract the foot back to the on-guard stance. Do not leave the leg out there (see Figs 159–160).

Fig 161. Stand in a neutral stance looking to your right.

Fig 162. Raise the right knee.

Fig 163. Pivot on the supporting foot as you side kick.

Exercise for the Stationary Side Kick

From a neutral stance with the feet shoulder-width apart, look to the right. Raise the right knee with the leg turned slightly to the right, then pivot on the other foot as you extend the leg out to side kick (see Figs 161–163).

The Stationary Front Kick

From the on-guard stance, use a snapping motion from the knee to make contact with the instep of the foot to the groin. (see Figs 164–165). Alternatively, use the ball of the foot to strike the mid-section of the body with a thrust from the hip. Make sure the kick is retracted quickly so the opponent has no chance to catch your leg (see Fig 166).

Fig 164. On-guard facing an opponent.

Fig 165. Instep kick to the groin.

Fig 166. Thrust kick with ball of the foot to mid-level.

The Lead Scoop Kick

The lead scoop kick is used when you are close in to an opponent. It consists of raising the knee and scooping the groin with the instep of the foot. It can be used as a counter to an opponent immobilizing your lead arm to strike or in combination with an attempt to trap an opponent's arms (see Figs 167–169).

Fig 167. In the midst of trapping.

Fig 170. On-guard facing an opponent.

Fig 171. Lead leg moves over to left kicking runway.

Fig 168. Scoop kick to groin.

Fig 169. Pulling the foot back.

Fig 172. Inverted hook kick.

The Inverted Hook Kick

From the right lead on-guard stance, the lead foot travels onto the rear leg runway in an arcing motion and curves into the target. The area of the foot used to strike can be the instep or the point of the shoe. Once again, a good target is the groin or higher, at the solar plexus. The inverted hook works well against an unmatched lead opponent curving around the opponent's lead leg (see Figs 170–172).

The Rear Leg Oblique Kick

The target for the rear leg oblique kick is the shin or the knee of an opponent's lead leg. The rear leg is swung out along the rear leg runway and strike the opponent with the heel or arch of your foot using a stiff leg (see Figs 173–174).

Fig 173. On-guard facing an opponent.

Fig 174. Rear leg oblique kick.

Fig 175. Facing an opponent in on-guard stance.

Fig 176. Opponent slides his rear foot up incorrectly, telegraphing his intentions...

Fig 177. ...leaving himself open for a stop-kick.

Kicking from a Distance

To kick an opponent you have to be close enough to reach the target with the required kick. Often, though, you will find yourself outside this kicking range. Remember, if you can reach an opponent with a kick he can also reach you. So, when sparring, one tends to stand outside of this range (see Chapter 4, Fighting Measure). To bring yourself into kicking distance requires a seamless blending of footwork with kicking.

By stepping into the area between yourself and an opponent (no man's land) you run the risk of being intercepted, so a form of distraction is required. In the case of a lead hook kick from long range the lead hand will move first, faking a lead finger jab (see Chapter 4, Finger Jab Biu-Jee). This will deceive an opponent whilst you are able to slide up the rear foot to the lead foot. This movement is like the first part of the slide step (see Chapter 3). The knees remain slightly bent, maintaining the lower centre of gravity. The lead leg is now in range to fire the lead hook kick. The lead hand fake also helps to overcome initial inertia from a stationary bai-jong by pulling the body forward.

In order to keep the kick non-telegraphic it is important not to pivot and roll the hips over until after the rear foot steps up. The lead leg is already travelling on the kicking runway before the pivot of the rear foot. If you pivot the rear foot before the lead leg is on the way you will telegraph the kick. Worse still is to pivot the foot from long range before you even slide up the rear foot. This will leave you wide open for interception on the preparation to kick (see Figs 175–177).

Exercise to Improve Kicking

From the on-guard position, raise the rear leg into the air and swing it down in a pendulum action. Swing the lead leg forward as the rear leg takes its place. This exercise will help to increase the speed of the kick and improve the

Fig 178. Raise the rear leg in the air.

Fig 179. Pendulum through to kick.

transition through the point where both feet come together. You do not want to be caught standing with both feet together – this is like standing on the head of a pin (see Figs 178–179).

The Whip Principle and the Water Principle

A combination of the whip and water principle can improve the explosiveness of a kick. Have a training partner hold a focus pad to receive a side kick. First, snap out a side kick barely touching the focus pad and whip it back as fast as you can – the whip principle. Now fire the side kick with deep penetration, driving the leg straight through the target like water rushing out of a water hose – the water principle. Now switch between these two methods. The goal is to find, through experimentation, the optimum position between the two movements to give the best explosive impact.

The Leg Obstruction

Although the leg obstruction is not really considered a kick, it is used to prevent an opponent from intercepting you as you close the fighting measure distance to strike. By raising the lead foot from the ground and turning the blade of the foot sidewards, you take up a stiff-legged position that jams up the opponent's low line, preventing him from kicking or moving forward. As you raise the lead leg, the hips are twisted sharply squaring up the shoulders, chambering the lead hand ready to fire on the runway (see Figs 180–182).

Another way to apply the leg obstruction is to raise the leg straight up, striking with the ball of the foot just under the kneecap. This has a jarring effect on an opponent's lead leg, making it not only a cover of the low line, but also a painful distraction, clearing the way for a strong hand attack (see Figs 183–185).

Fig 180. The leg obstruction.

Fig 183. On-guard facing an opponent.

Fig 181. On-guard facing an opponent.

Fig 182. The leg obstruction.

Fig 184. Leg obstruction with the ball of the foot.

Fig 185. To a lead straight.

7   Interception

The literal translation of the Cantonese words 'Jeet Kune Do' is 'Way of the Intercepting Fist'. This gives a clear indication of the importance of the principle of interception. Interception is the highest form of defence, being the most direct way to counter-fight an opponent. Although almost any offensive tool can be used to intercept, Jeet Kune Do leans towards the use of the lead hand and lead foot. This is because of the structure of the bai-jong on-guard stance and adherence to the principle of 'longest weapon to the closest target.'

The Stop-Hit

The term used for interception in Jeet Kune Do is the 'stop-hit' borrowed from Western fencing, the idea being to stop the opponent during his attack or on his preparation to attack.

If you are controlling the fighting measure, then your opponent will need to step in to be in range to hit you. This step in is considered to be his preparation. If you use a stop-kick at this point you will stop an opponent in his tracks, setting yourself up for follow-up attacks (see Figs 186–187).

Interception on an opponent's preparation requires control of distance, good timing and a heightened sense of awareness if you are going to respond instantly. It is important to learn to read an opponent, as his movements can 'telegraph' his intentions to attack. If an opponent pulls back his arm chambering to punch, he should have already been hit. To do this you will sometimes have to take a step forward or at least lean in to be able to land a solid hit first (see Figs 188–189).

The second way to intercept is during an opponent's attack. This means the attacking

Fig 186. Facing an opponent.

Fig 187. As the opponent lunges in, you counter with a stop-kick.

Fig 188. The opponent appears aggressive.

Fig 189. The opponent pulls his arm back to punch and is intercepted.

Fig 190. On-guard facing an opponent.

Fig 191. Stop-kick counters a rear round kick.

tool is already on its way in. In the case of an opponent kicking you it is possible to 'attack the attack' with a kick of your own. This requires you to raise your leg aggressively in the line of the opponent's kick (see Figs 190–191).

It is sometimes necessary to back up the stop-hit with slipping to evade his line of attack, or to back up the hit with a cover as shown in the pictures below (see Figs 192–193).

Fig 192. Bird's-eye view of on-guard.

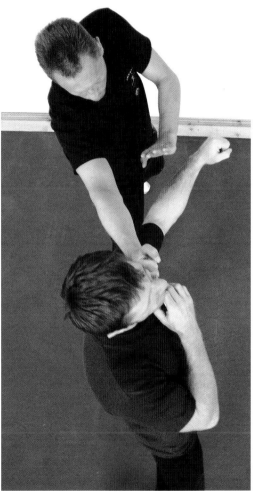

Fig 193. Time-hit with rear cover.

Fig 194. On-guard facing an opponent.

Fig 195. Rear hand parry against the jab.

Fig 196. Hit on the half beat as opponent pulls back his hand to lead hook.

Half Beat Timing

It is possible to intercept the moves of an opponent's combination attack. This requires a stop-hit on the half beat. To understand this you need to see the opponent's attack as a rhythm. A combination of a jab-cross-hook would be 1-2-3. Between the 1 and 2 is a half beat, and also between the 2 and 3 is a half beat. So if the rhythm becomes 1 and 2 and 3 you would need to hit on either 'and'. This small window of opportunity gives you the chance to intercept an opponent in the midst of his attack (see Figs 194–196).

Time-Hit

The time-hit is a stop-hit that bridges across the opponent's attacking limb as he attacks using the built-in wedge principle of the bai-jong on-guard stance. To intercept with a time-hit is a great way to break down the structure of the opponent's stance as you crash through, breaking his balance and opening up his centre line for further attack (see Figs 197–198).

Fig 197. On-guard facing an opponent.

Fig 198. Time-hit against the jab.

Exercises for the Time-Hit

Facing a training partner, have him feed a steady diet of straight punches while you practise bridging both inside and outside using the built-in wedge principle (see Diagrams 1–2).

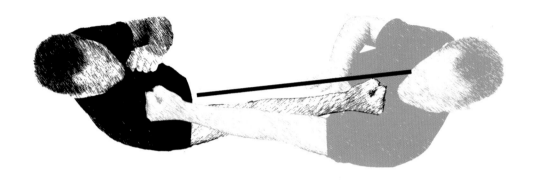

Diagram 1. Inside bridge punch.

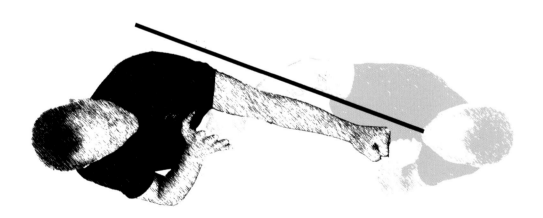

Diagram 2. Outside bridge punch.

8 The Five Ways of Attack

There are only five ways for an opponent to attack you or for you to attack him. When broken down, most attacks will fall into one of the following categories, or a combination of some or all of the five.

- Simple attacks: Single direct attack (SDA) or single angulated attack (SAA)
- Attack by combination (ABC)
- Progressive indirect attack (PIA)
- Hand immobilization attack (HIA)
- Attack by drawing (ABD)
(see Diagram 3).

Although the five ways can be categorized as separate entities, when combined there are a variety of attacks available which can flow one into the other. The ability to flow effortlessly from one way to another at a split second's notice, taking advantage of the opponent's weakness, is the key to controlling the fight (see Diagram 4).

The success of the attack often depends on the type of opponent you face. Does he try to intercept your every move, does he block and hit or try to jam up your every attack? Does he always try to control the distance, waiting for an opportune moment to hit? Is he a runner backing way out of distance at every attempt you make to hit? Does he try to clinch up with you or is he always shooting in to try to take you down? An opponent could be a combination of any of these types of fighter at any time during the encounter. Having command of the five ways of attack allows you to adapt, flow and fit in with the opponent. Sometimes an opponent's style of movement will dictate

Diagram 3. Five ways of attack.

Diagram 4. Combinations.

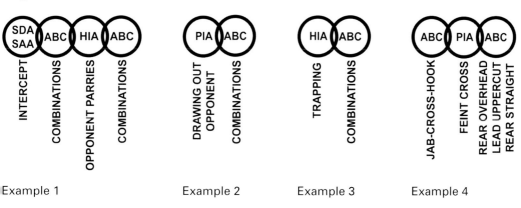

Fig 199. The opponent is uncovered.

Fig 200. Single direct hit.

your choice of technique. When sparring, it is important to be switched on at all times so you can see and feel an opponent's actions in the midst of his movement and learn to recognize how he reacts to your attacks. The following is a break down of the five ways of attack.

Simple Attacks

Single Direct Attack (SDA)

The single direct attack (SDA) is a single motion that travels directly to the target with no intention to conceal it. The single direct attack relies on correct timing, speed and economy of motion. It can be used as a stop-hit as the opponent prepares to attack, or to beat him to the punch in the midst of his combination. A good time to fire a single direct attack is that moment when the oppo-

nent is 'not there', the point when his mind has wandered. If he switches off for a fraction of a second he should have been hit. If an opponent continually leaves a target unintentionally open, fill in that space with a single direct attack (see Figs 199–200).

The SDA has the best chance of arriving at its target as an opponent is opening a line of attack rather than closing it. Another good time to launch a single direct attack is when an opponent is returning to his on-guard stance after a missed shot, leaving a hole in his defence.

Single Angulated Attack (SAA)

The single angulated attack is a variation of the single direct attack. It is still a single movement but is thrown from an unexpected angle by shifting the body to the side or taking a step to create an opening in an opponent's defence (see Figs 201–202).

Fig 201. Facing an opponent.

Fig 202. Single angular attack against a jab.

Attack by Combination (ABC)

Attack by combination consists of two or more offensive tools thrown at an opponent. All the strikes are intended to hit specific targets and should blend smoothly together in a natural flow. There are many ways of linking tools together, using hands, feet, elbows and knees. Below are some examples.

Lead Hand to Lead Hand Combinations
- Lead jab to lead hook
- Lead jab to lead uppercut
- Lead jab to lead jab
- High jab to low jab
- Low jab to high jab
- Low jab to lead hook
- High jab to lead body hook

Lead Hand to Rear Hand Combinations
- Jab to cross
- Jab to rear uppercut
- Jab to rear overhead
- Lead hook to cross
- Lead uppercut to cross
- Lead uppercut to rear overhead

Lead Foot to Lead Hand Combinations
- Lead hook kick to lead straight
- Lead hook kick to lead backfist

Lead Hand to Rear Foot Combinations
- Lead jab to rear round kick
- Lead jab to rear oblique kick

Lead Foot to Lead Foot Combinations
- Front kick to hook kick
- Front kick to inverted hook kick
- Hook kick to hook kick

Lead Foot to Rear Foot Combinations
- Front kick to oblique kick
- Front kick to rear round kick

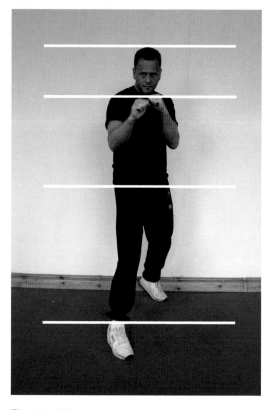

Fig 203. High, mid and low areas of attack.

Rear Foot to Lead Foot Combinations
- Rear oblique kick to lead hook kick
- Rear oblique kick to side kick

Three-Count Combinations
- Jab-cross-hook
- Jab-cross-lead uppercut
- Jab-cross-body hook
- Jab-lead hook-cross
- Jab-lead hook-rear uppercut
- Jab-lead hook-rear overhead
- Cross-hook-cross
- Cross-lead uppercut-cross
- Rear overhead-lead uppercut-rear overhead
- Lead uppercut-rear overhead-lead uppercut

Fig 204. Side view of high, mid and low areas of attack.

It is important to have knowledge of all anatomical targets so that you can vary attacks to different lines. The body is divided into three areas or lines of attack: the high-line, the mid-line and the low-line. An attack in one line often leaves another line open. (see Figs 203–204).

ABC with Broken Rhythm

A variation of the attack by combination is to break up the rhythmic flow by adding a pause or a stutter. Take a four-count combination: jab-cross-hook-cross. Regulate the beat or pulse of the tools so they are all equal in speed of delivery: jab-cross-hook-cross. Now add in the pause: jab-pause-cross-hook-cross, jab-cross-pause-hook-cross, jab-cross-hook-pause-cross.

Another variation on this would be to either speed up or slow down the delivery of the tools, for example:

Jab	Cross	Hook	Cross
Fast	Fast	Fast	Fast
Slow	Fast	Fast	Fast
Slow	Fast	Slow	Fast
Fast	Fast	Slow	Fast

Note that the last shot is always fast. Breaking the rhythm of the various components of the combination during an attack (pausing, slowing down or speeding up) helps to break down an opponent's defence. This can leave an opponent either overreacting or reacting too late to the strikes.

Feints, Fakes and False Attacks in ABC

Feints, fakes and false attacks are designed to provoke a reaction from an opponent.

Feints

Feints are used to open a line of attack. By feeding only half of the attacking tool you can deceive the opponent. Feints should be regulated to an opponent's reaction speed. If done too fast you may not draw the anticipated reaction and end up firing the next shot into a closed line. If, on the other hand, your feint is held too long an opponent may just counterstrike before you change the attack.

Correct distance is also a deciding factor when feinting. If the feint is too close an opponent may simply intercept you. It is also a good idea to be well covered just in case an opponent does not take the bait and just hits back.

Fakes

Fakes are also designed to open a line of attack by giving some hint of the tool that you are going to throw, shifting the body in a

Fig 205. On-guard facing an opponent.

Fig 206. False attack falls short...

way that appears to show which tool you are about to fire. You can fake with almost any part of the body – shoulder, head, waist and knees. Even the eyes can distract an opponent's attention.

False Attack

A false attack travels deeper than a feint but falls short of the target. This is a real attack that gains a reaction from an opponent. The attack may even touch an opponent with no force behind it. This is known as a 'negative' shot designed to set up a 'positive' knock-out blow (see Figs 205–207).

Fig 207. ...to set up a knock-out blow.

Progressive Indirect Attack (PIA)

Progressive indirect attack is also known as a 'second intention attack,' meaning the second part of the action is intended to hit, the first part being the feint to 'set up' the opponent. The progressive indirect attack is used against an opponent who has a strong defence and is difficult to hit with a single direct attack.

'Progressive' refers to the distance covered. The feint should cover half of the distance towards the opponent, and the other half is for real and is intended to hit. Correct distance is crucial. If the feint is made too close to the opponent there is a chance that you will be hit with his counter-attack. If the feint is from too great a distance, you may get no reaction from your opponent at all. The feint must be held long enough for the opponent to react to it.

'Indirect' covers time. The idea is to be ahead of an opponent's defensive parry or block. It should feel like the opponent is 'blocking air' as your tool changes to another

Fig 208. On-guard facing an opponent.

line. It is most important that there is no retraction of the feint and everything continues to travel forwards.

Most attacks usually fall into a steady rhythmical beat, for example one and two and three. The speed of this rhythm can vary from opponent to opponent. The idea of the progressive indirect attack is to strike on the half beat, the feint being on the 'one' beat in

Fig 211. Facing an opponent.

Fig 212. Low straight (feint)...

Fig 209. Feint high...

Fig 210. ...to low jab with no retraction of the tool.

time and the actual strike occurring on the half beat. Therefore the strike is on the 'and' of the rhythm. This is a window of opportunity for an attack. As an opponent moves towards your feint to defend, you strike on the half beat in the opening line with no retraction of the weapon.

Progressive indirect attacks can be done in many ways. Here are some examples.

Fig 213. ...to curve.

Lead Hand to Lead Hand
- High straight to mid straight (see Figs 208–210)
- Mid straight to high straight
- Mid straight to high curve (two ways) (see Figs 211–213).

Hand to Foot
- Straight to straight

Foot to Hand
- Straight to straight

Foot to Foot
- Straight to curve
- Curve to straight

Front Hand to Rear Hand
- Straight to straight

When using a progressive indirect attack, make sure you take care of your own defence. Keep well covered as you move into the real attack because your opponent may give the impression of reacting to your feint, thus setting up his counter-attack on your attack.

Fig 214. On-guard facing an opponent.

Fig 215. Crashing in with a pak-sau chung-chuie.

Immobilization Attack (IA)

Immobilization attack is the trapping or the pinning of a part of an opponent's body, immobilizing it in order to hit in an open line. It is also used to force the opponent to defend in a way that makes his position vulnerable and open to an attack

There are different ways to immobilize an opponent, the most common being the hand immobilization attack (HIA). This involves trapping one or both of the opponent's arms, preventing him from moving his arm, or arms, whilst you hit through the open line. Hand immobilization attack can be used by design as a 'set-up' in combination with the other ways of attack, forcing an opponent to react in a certain way, or as a follow-up to an opponent's natural defensive patterns. Hand immobilization attack is also a way to close down an opponent's attempts to stop-hit when you bridge the gap (see Figs 214–215).

It is also a useful way to close the gap safely on an opponent who parries at the same time as retreating just outside of your punching range (see Figs 216–218).

Fig 216. On-guard facing an opponent.

Fig 217. Step in and jab – the opponent slides back and parries.

Fig 218. Close the gap with a pak-sau qua-chuie.

Reference Points

Reference point trapping is simply a place for a beginner to start immobilization training from. There are three basic positions: outside high, inside high and low outside.

Outside High Stand facing a training partner in the on-guard position and extend your lead arm along the runway until you cross arms at the partner's wrist area, with your arm turned in on a 45-degree angle. The pronation of your forearm keeps your defensive structure intact during an attack. The correct distance to work from is one from where it is not possible to strike an opponent's face without using push-shuffle footwork to close the gap (see Figs 219–220).

Inside High The only difference between this and the high outside position is that the inside high position has inside forearm contact. Everything else remains the same (see Fig 221).

Low Outside When facing a partner for the low outside reference, bend your knees to simulate a low lead straight to the body whilst crossing the partner's lead hand wrist on the low line (see Fig 222).

Tools for Trapping

The basic tools for trapping are pak-sau, lop-sau, jut-sau, jau-sau and huen-sau.

Fig 219. High outside reference point.

Fig 220. Incorrect high outside reference point.

Fig 221. Inside high reference point.

Fig 222. Low outside reference point.

Fig 223. High outside reference point.

Fig 224. Pak-sau chung-chuie.

Fig 225. Inside high reference point.

Fig 226. Pak-sau qua-chuie (backfist).

Fig 227. Low outside reference point.

Fig 228. Pak-sau qua-chuie.

Fig 229. Facing an opponent.

Fig 230. Pak-sau chung chuie from non-attachment.

Pak-Sau

Pak-sau is the immobilization of an opponent's arm using a cupped hand called a 'slap hand'. Although the target area is just below the elbow, it can also vary from below the elbow, on the tricep and up to the shoulder depending on the situation. The pak-sau from the high reference point is referred to as 'from the nucleus in' and is known as an attachment (see Figs 223–224).

Moving out from the nucleus is known as trapping from non-attachment. This requires fast, explosive footwork and hand speed to crash into an opponent's limb, not only trapping his arm but also breaking his structure and balance (see Figs 229–230).

Finally, you can also use a leg obstruction to close the gap from a greater range, then immobilize an opponent's arm as you step down to hit (see Figs 231–233).

Fig 231. Facing an opponent.

Fig 232. Closing the gap with a foot obstruction.

Fig 233. To pak-sau chung-chuie.

Lop-Sau

Lop-sau is the grabbing hand. It pulls an opponent into your hit at the same time as breaking his balance and creating a whiplash effect to the neck. From the high outside reference point, slide your arm forward using a biu-jee finger jab motion. At the same time, allow the lead hip to twist forward, then snap the hand back, grabbing his wrist as you turn your hip back in the opposite direction. You only need to pull your opponent's arm enough to open the line of attack (see Figs 234–236).

Fig 234. High reference point.

Fig 237. Opponent covers lead straight.

Fig 238. Jut-sau chung-chuie.

Fig 235. Biu-jee finger jab.

Fig 236. Lop-sau chung-chuie.

Fig 239. To lead straight.

Jut-Sau

Jut-sau is the jerking hand, used when an opponent jams up the line of attack. Using a cupped hand, jerk his arm down to break his defensive cover. The jut-sau fits in really well with the timed hits and the straight blast (see Figs 237–239).

Fig 240. High reference point.

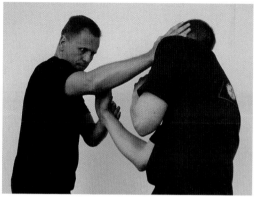

Fig 241. Jau-sau.

Jau-Sau

Jau-sau is the running hand. This is a large disengagement from the high outside line, circling in a 'U' shape to the outside of an opponent's rear arm, striking with a heel palm to the jaw or ear. It is important to cover an opponent's lead arm when making the disengagement with your rear hand so that you do not run into his lead straight punch. Remember the jau-sau is a strike and not just a means of attachment to an opponent's rear hand (see Figs 240–241).

Huen-Sau

Huen-Sau is a small disengagement made with a wrist circle from high outside to high inside. Make sure you cover the opponent's lead hand with your rear hand as you make the small disengagement (see Figs 242–244).

Fig 242. High reference.

Fig 243. Huen-sau, small disengagement...

Fig 244. ...to biu-jee with rear hand cover.

When to Trap and When to Hit

Remember the purpose of the trap is to hit.
Do not trap for the sake of trapping. Most
times it is possible to hit instead of trap. If an
opponent holds his ground and defends with
an inside block against your lead hand strike,
he is still in range to be hit. Using half-beat
timing, you should simply hit him with a rear
chung-chuie or rear straight (see Figs
245–247).

Fig 245. On-guard facing an opponent.

Fig 246. Opponent holds his ground and blocks.

Fig 247. Rear straight.

If an opponent slides back at the same time as he parries, he opens up the fighting measure. At this range you cannot hit an opponent with the rear hand without taking a step towards him and if you step you stand a good chance of walking into an opponent's counter-attack. This is the right time to explode forwards using the push-shuffle footwork and close the line down with the pak-sau (see Figs 248–250).

In this second scenario, step in with a lead hand strike to the chin, which the opponent parries with his rear hand. This opens a window on the outside for a rear chung-chuie to slide through. Using the wedge principle, your left hand slides through on the outside of the opponent's left arm. If the opponent jams up this line of attack so that you cannot feed the strike through, pull back with the lop-sau to remove the barrier and strike with the right chung-chuie (see Figs 251–254).

Fig 248. On guard facing opponent.

Fig 251. On-guard facing an opponent.

Fig 252. Opponent parries with his rear hand.

Fig 249. Opponent slides back, parrying the jab.

Fig 250. Close the gap with a pak-sau chung-chuie.

Fig 253. The rear chung-chuie is jammed.

Fig 254. Lop-sau chung-chuie.

Trapping – Key Points

- Trap with the whole body and not just the hand.
- Borrow energy from the ground using the push off the rear leg's ball of the foot.
- Do not trap simply for the sake of trapping.
- The purpose of the trap is to HIT!

Hair/Head Immobilization

It is possible to control or immobilize an opponent by grabbing his hair. Pulling the hair tends to move the head in the direction of the pull, and where the head moves the body will follow. This technique can be very effective and painful, especially when the hair is pulled against the natural direction of growth.

Foot Immobilization Attack (FIA)

Foot immobilization attack can be used in several ways. The most straightforward way to use this form of attack is to step on an opponent's foot. By doing this you can stop him retreating as you strike. Care must be taken when training in this form of immobilization as it is easy to damage your partner's ankle as he tries to pull his foot away.

Leg Immobilization Attack

It is also possible to jam up an opponent's lead leg as you step in close to him by placing your lead foot inside his lead foot and applying pressure to his leg with your shin. This makes an opponent's knee joint lock out, breaking down his structure.

Attack by Drawing (ABD)

Like progressive indirect attack, attack by drawing is a form of deception. In this case, you are opening up a line of attack to invite an opponent in. This can be done by opening, closing, raising or lowering one arm or the other (see Figs 255–259).

This must be done in a way that makes an opponent see that there is a weakness in your cover that you are not aware of. Once he

Fig 255. On-guard.

Fig 256. Lowering the lead hand.

Fig 257. Lowering the rear hand.

commits to the attack in the open line, you pounce. This is a form of 'baiting' and it has to be convincing enough to make him take the bite. If you make it too obvious he will know it is a trap. Once again, timing and distance play a major part here. If you open a line from too far away, an opponent will not try to reach you. On the other hand, if you are too close, he may take the bait and hit you before you can get your intended attack in motion.

Another way to draw an opponent in is to keep faking the same shot several times. Each time you retract the tool, lower the arm so that an opponent can see that you are always uncovered when you return to the on-guard position. As he tries to capitalize on your mistake, use your counter-attack. You can also force an attack by moving towards an opponent with a line open, the closer you step into an opponent's comfort zone, the more likely it is that he will have to hit or be hit himself. This is a way of drawing the opponent's stop-hit so that you can parry or counter-hit. If you immobilize the opponent's lead arm, it is possible to force him to fire the rear straight, then countering with the wedge principle to cut into his strike.

By step-slide retreating back you can draw an opponent to step forward to maintain fighting measure. As you keep stepping back, take smaller and smaller steps until he steps in too close, at which point you intercept him. This is a deceptive play on the fighting measure, striking the opponent on his lead step forward.

Fig 258. Opening the wedge. Fig 259. Closing the wedge.

9   Sensitivity

To gain an awareness of an opponent's energy and direction of force, the Jeet Kune Do practitioner trains in several sensitivity exercises. An ability to 'feel' an opponent's intention through contact reflex and the sense of touch allows him to react to the opponent's movement quickly.

At long range we have the ability to see an opponent's movement and have more time to react but this distance can be closed very quickly. At a closer range it takes too long for us to send a message from the eyes to the brain and down to the limbs in time to defend successfully, hence the development of contact reflexes. The ability to control an opponent's limbs when in close proximity is a vital part of your attack and defence.

In closing the gap between yourself and an opponent, it is often necessary to trap or immobilize one of the opponent's arms. At this point of contact, an opponent may react in many different ways. He can freeze up, tensing his arm, he may try to disengage his arm from the trap or just hit out with his free hand. All these reactions can be picked up sooner with a heightened tactile awareness.

Fig 260. Unmatched leads.

Fig 261. Left bong-sau, right chung-chuie.

In attempting to shut down an opponent's attacking tools, you will force an opponent to react in a certain way. This is when the ability to feel an opponent's intentions will keep you ahead of his attack.

Most of the sensitivity drills in Jeet Kune Do have been modified from old Wing Chun gung fu exercises to fit in with the bai-jong on-guard stance.

Dan Chi-Sau: Single-Hand Sticking

Single-hand sticking is often overlooked by students who are eager to get onto the double-hand method. Its importance lies in the fact that the Jeet Kune Do practitioner stands strong side forward. In the case of right lead versus left lead the hands often replicate the position of the dan chi-sau drill (see Fig 260).

Right Lead Versus Left Lead

The dan-chi exercise consists of various hand positions and their counterparts. The example shown here is a right lead versus left lead bai-jong. The starting position is right side, the right chung-chuie straight punch deflected by the left bong-sau wing arm (see Fig 261).

The left bong-sau drops the elbow down into a tan-sau palm-up position. This is

Fig 262. Left tan-sau, right fook-sau.

Fig 263. Left palm strike, right jum-sau.

covered with the right fook-sau bridging hand (see Fig 262). The left palm strike to the solar plexus is covered with a jum-sau sinking arm (see Fig 263). From the jum-sau position on the right you can continue with a chung-chuie front punch and the cycle continues back and forth (see Fig 263).

Included in the dan-chi drill are disen-gagements. These are high to low and low to high. Feint the punch high and disen-gage to a mid-level punch (see Figs 264–265).

Feint a low palm strike to disengage and punch high (see Figs 266–267).

Fig 264. Fake chung-chuie...

Fig 265. ...to low punch covered with left jum-sau.

Fig 266. Fake palm strike...

Fig 267. ...to chung-chuie covered with bong-sau.

Also apply huen-sau, circling the hand to change from inside to outside position or from outside to inside position. From the tan-sau palm-up position, huen-sau circle the hand underneath to chung-chuie front punch, which is covered by a bong-sau wing arm (see Figs 268–270).

Or, from the fook-sau bridging hand, huen-sau circle inside to bong-sau wing arm as the other side feeds a chung-chuie front punch (see Figs 271–273).

The dan-chi exercise is somewhat like two western fencers at engagement, blades touching and both trying to feel each other's pressure on the blade, and both seeking to disengage and strike in an open line. When practising dan-chi single-hand sticking in the bai-jong on-guard stance, be sure to keep the rear hand up to protect the face and ready to be used as a back-up hand when you strike.

Fig 268. Fook-sau covers tan-sau.

Fig 271. Left tan-sau covered by right fook-sau.

Fig 269. Transition huen-sau under.

Fig 270. To right chung-chuie covered by left bong-sau.

Fig 272. Transition huen-sau over.

Fig 273. To left chung-chuie right bong-sau.

Lop-Sau Exercise

Using the lop, or grabbing hand, in combination with the bong-sau wing arm is a means of deflecting or dissolving energy. It is a continuous rolling cycle of bong-sau lop-sau against a chung-chuie punch.

Right Lead Versus Left Lead

Start with a right bong-sau position deflecting a left chung-chuie punch (see Fig 274).

The right side person grabs his partner's left punch with a lop-sau grabbing hand and rolls his right bong-sau into a chung-chuie punch. As the person on the left feels this, he immediately changes his left arm into a bong-sau wing arm (see Figs 275–276).

Fig 274. Right bong-sau deflecting a left chung-chuie.

Fig 275. Lap-sau grabbing hand.

Fig 276. To right chung-chuie deflected by a left bong-sau.

Fig 277. Transition, lap-sau...

Fig 278. ...to left chung-chuie, right bong-sau.

Fig 279. Left chung-chuie, right bong-sau.

Fig 280. To lop-sau sat-sau knife hand.

The cycle is then continued back and forth (see Figs 277–278). While working on this drill there are many hand changes that can take place, so you can switch the drill from the left side to the right side and also add in various attacks that, if defended well, will also allow you to change sides. An example of a change from one side to the other is illustrated here (see Figs 279–281).

Fig 281. To lop-sau chung-chuie covered with bong-sau.

Fig 282. Left ding-sau fook-sau, right bong-sau, left tan-sau.

Fig 283. Left fook-sau, right ding-sau, right tan-sau, left bong-sau.

Fig 284. Left ding-sau, right tan-sau, right bong-sau, left fook-sau.

Fig 285. Left fook-sau, right bong-sau right tan-sau, left ding-sau.

Fig 286. Left bong-sau, right tan-sau, right ding-sau, left fook-sau.

Chi-Sau: Double-Hand Sticking

In the double hand sticking drill, the Jeet Kune Do practitioner strives to develop a forward flowing energy. This is done by both partners attaching themselves to each other's arms and rolling in harmony, as well as in contrast. Both sides will try to equalize the forward pressure. If one side feels a pause or weakness in the flow of energy then he will automatically shoot the limb forward in the form of an attack, like water bursting through the smallest crack in a dam. Imagine two connected hose pipes with water being forced in from both ends and meeting in the middle, creating an intense pressure there. When your arms are attached to a partner's arms in this fashion they become spring-like because of the matching opposing pressure. Your arms become sensitive to the pressure, feeling any change, be it less or more. If an opponent's limb tries to break through your defence, either apply more pressure to your arm so it acts as a break to the opponent's strike or, if his pressure is too much, dissolve his force, deflecting his energy from the desired target and returning with a strike of your own.

The first stage in chi-sau is called seung chi-sau. This is the training in the different hand positions and establishing the rolling cycle with flowing energy. There are several basic positions to practise the rolling hands from (see Figs 282–286).

While rolling through these positions, the pressure must be kept even so that there is no gap in each turn and roll. Try not to turn the rolling hands into a jerky arm wrestling match. The idea of chi-sau is simply to develop a flowing energy whilst rotating the arms.

The second stage is called jeung-sau. At this stage the rolling positions are blended by changing hand position in the midst of the flow. Although hands are rolled in harmony, each hand starts to move and react independently of the other.

The third stage is called the dok-sau. This stage introduces simple attacks and their counters and involves hand immobilization skills.

The fourth stage is called gor-sau. In this stage, rolling hand positions are used as a starting reference. This allows freedom of attack or defence in a freelance manner with no fixed movement. In other words, it is time to try and score on a partner by feeling for weaknesses in his defensive structure.

The fifth stage is called chi-sau leung-bye-muk. One partner is now blindfolded and consequently develops an even higher level of tactile awareness without the use of his eyes (see Fig 287).

Fig 287. Blindfold chi-sau.

Harmonious Spring Drill

The harmonious spring drill helps to develop the skill of bridging an opponent's arm by sliding forward on the inside of a partner's arm or cutting into the tool on the outside. It also allows for the deflection of force on the inside with a tan-sau palm-up block, or on the outside with a bong-sau wing arm.

Right Lead Versus Left Lead

The left arm touches the outside of a partner's right wrist. The left arm applies a jut-sau jerking hand, pulling the right arm down, and returning with a chung-chuie (see Figs 288–290).

As the left hand punches, the right hand responds with spring energy to any of the counters available (see Figs 291–294).

Fig 288. Unmatched leads with left arm outside reference.

Fig 291. Inside biu-jee.

Fig 292. Outside bridge punch.

Fig 289. Jut-sau.

Fig 290. Chung-chuie.

Fig 293. Bong-sau.

Fig 294. Tan-sau.

Swinging Gate Drill

The swinging gate exercise helps to train the beginner in dissolving energy on the inside or the outside of your arm.

Face your partner and place your right hand on his right shoulder. The partner then knocks your right hand away with his left forearm. Counter this by bending your arm inwards at the elbow, grabbing his wrist with your left hand and firing a qua-chuie backfist. This is known as the 'bamboo' principle, as, like bamboo, your arm gives way to the pressure of an outside force until it slides off, creating a spring-loaded effect as your arm returns back to its original position. In this case you return back with a strike (see Figs 295–297).

Fig 295. The right hand touches the opponent's left shoulder.

Fig 296. Inside forearm wipe-off.

Fig 297. Lop-sau chung-chuie.

Fig 298. Right-hand touch to left shoulder, inside wipe-off.

Fig 299. Pak-sau.

Face your partner and touch his left shoulder with your right hand. The partner then knocks off your right arm with an inside right sweep of his arm. Dissolve his energy by using the 'ball and socket' principle. The ball and socket of the shoulder joint opens out slightly and rotates inwards to allow the forearm to roll inwards as you trap his arm with a left pak-sau slap hand. Your right arm continues forward to strike with a qua-chuie backfist (see Figs 298–300).

Fig 300. Qua-chuie.

Pak-Sau Reflex Drills

The pak-sau reflex drills are exercises developed at the Impact Martial Arts Academy. These drills were developed to help students to study the hand immobilization attack whilst advancing and retreating with footwork. They also help develop good defensive skills whilst retreating. The drills cover all possible lines of engagement in hand immobilization attack on a moving opponent (see Figs 301–307).

Fig 301. High reference.

Fig 302. Pak-sau chung-chuie.

Fig 305. The other side returns pak-sau chung-chuie.

Fig 306. Inside pak-sau chung-chuie.

Fig 303. Inside pak-sau chung-chuie.

Fig 304. Low reference.

Fig 307. Back to low reference.

Fig 308. High reference.

Fig 309. Lop-sau chung-chuie.

Fig 312. Transition to the other side.

Fig 313. Lop-sau chung-chuie.

Lop-Sau Reflex Drills

These exercises are designed to develop the skills of the lop-sau grabbing hand on both the outside and the inside of an opponent's arm, feeling the pressure of an opponent's energy and reacting accordingly (see Figs 308–315).

The goal of all of the sensitivity and reflex drills is to allow you to develop skills in tactile awareness. Most drills have three stages:

Stage 1 Learn the exercise
Stage 2 Abide by the exercise
Stage 3 Dissolve the exercise

Fig 310. Rear lop-sau chung-chuie.

Fig 311. Inside lop-sau qua-chuie.

Fig 314. Rear lop-sau chung-chuie.

Fig 315. Inside lop-sau chung-chuie.

Dissolving in this case does not mean to throw away. It means you no longer have to think about what to do, 'it' just happens.

A good way to apply this is to have a sparring session that focuses on chi-sau sticking energy. The round has to be fought close range and includes clinching. The time has come to leave the rolling hands and instead apply the skills developed from the exercises. The round should include single and double attachments, disengagements, neck control and simultaneous neck and arm controls and breakouts. This develops applied sensitivity that stops you from becoming bound by the rolling hand drills.

141

10   Grappling

The world of grappling is so vast that it would take several books alone to cover this area but because the of the all-encompassing nature of Jeet Kune Do, it is important to cover this area. No slice of the pie should be left out.

In Jeet Kune Do the study of grappling can be divided into two main areas, standing and on the ground, each then further broken down into its various components. Standing grappling is often referred to as 'the clinch'.

The Clinch

At a casual glance the clinch looks like two fighters just clinging onto each other but to the initiated it presents a totally different picture – a picture of two opponents jockeying for superior position in order to strike or take each other down.

The Head Clinch

The head clinch is also known as the thai-plum. Here you retain close-in control of an opponent's head with both of your hands in a palm-down grip, keeping your elbows in and pulling the opponent's head down to your sternum (see Fig 316).

This is a dangerous position to be caught in. It leaves you open to multiple knee strikes to the head, body, legs and groin. It is imperative that you develop escapes from this position.

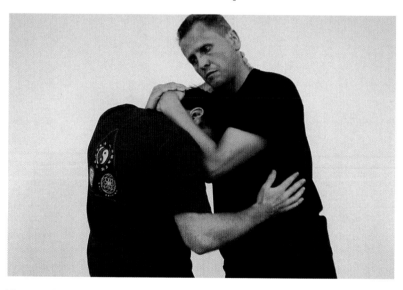

Fig 316. Double-hand head clinch.

Fig 317. Snake left arm in.

Fig 318. Snake right arm in back to double-hand head clinch.

Head Clinch Flow Drill

Start with a partner in a double neck clinch. Now feed one arm inside your partner's arm, snaking your hand behind the back of his head. Then feed the second arm inside, establishing the inside head clinch position. Do this drill back and forth, making sure to slide one arm in at a time so that you can still defend against attacks (see Figs 317–318).

50/50 Position

Both partners hold each other's necks with one hand and place the other hand in the crook of the elbow or under the arm at the tricep. Both sides are in an equal position.

Place your forehead on the opponent's shoulder to help defend against strikes. From this position try a range of close-in strikes – uppercuts, overheads and elbow strikes (see Fig 319).

Fig 319. The 50/50 position.

Fig 320. Both sides snake arm, left inside.

Fig 321. Switched to the other side.

50/50 Flow Drill

Both sides start in the 50/50 position. One side feeds the inside arm snake to get the head clinch. As the other side feels this he also slips his arm inside so that the 50/50 position is replaced on the other side. Both sides flow back and forth (see Figs 320–321).

Overhook/Underhook Clinch

In this position both sides underhook one arm and overhook the other arm. The overhooking arm goes over the partner's underhooking arm and holds his arms at the tricep. Make sure not to feed the underhook arm too far across the partner's back as this leaves the elbow susceptible to attack (see Fig 322).

Fig 322. Under and over hook position.

Fig 323. Both partners swim arms inside.

Fig 324. Switched to the other side.

The Overhook-Underhook Pummelling Flow Drill

Both partners start in the overhook/underhook clinch position. The goal is to change the overhook into an underhook. Both sides attempt this at the same time and in doing so reverse positions from side to side (see Figs 323–324).

From all of the above positions and drills there are numerous take-downs and throws.

Grappling on the Ground

In today's martial art world, although there are ways to stay on your feet and avoid the street tackle with superior footwork, a good sprawl and counters involving the hands, it is naïve to think that you will never be taken down to the ground (see Figs 325–327).

Against the seasoned grappler there is every chance that you will find yourself on the ground and if this is unfamiliar territory you will be in serious trouble. Obviously in a street situation, if you end up on the ground it should be a priority to get back onto your feet as fast as you can or reverse a bad position to a superior position so that you can counter-attack or escape.

Fig 325. The opponent shoots in.

Fig 326. For a single leg attack, slide leg back...

Fig 327. ...and sprawl.

There is a saying in the grappling world, 'Learn to be comfortable in uncomfortable positions'. The only way to achieve this is to immerse yourself in some form of grappling art in order to understand the strengths and weaknesses of each position. Let us take a look at some positions.

Do you know how to escape or counter all these positions (see Figs 328–329)?

Fig 328. Side control.

Fig 331. Opponent in your guard.

Fig 329. Knee ride.

Fig 330. Mount.

Fig 332. Rear mount, face down.

Fig 333. Rear mount, face up.

11 Training with Equipment

Equipment training plays a major role in the development of the Jeet Kune Do practitioner. It is important to keep an eye on the latest health and fitness developments in order to remain at the cutting edge of the martial arts. This includes checking out new training devices and new equipment as they appear on the market. Often it is the training that is done outside school that makes the difference. Supplementary training can include weights, resistance bands, cables, physio ball, kettle bells and medicine ball work. All of these will help your speed, power, explosive strength and endurance and help take your martial arts to the next level.

Some of the old training equipment in Jeet Kune Do that has stood the test of time are the focus gloves, the kick shield and the wooden dummy. They are just as important today as back in the time of the founder Bruce Lee.

Focus Gloves or Pads

The focus gloves are probably the most important and most valuable piece of training equipment available to the Jeet Kune Do practitioner. It is possible to train the entire repertoire of offensive and counter-offensive tools against a partner holding the gloves. Often the glove man is

Fig 334. Focus pads in the 'L' configuration.

Fig 335. Focus pads in 'V' configuration.

Fig 336. On-guard facing focus gloves.

Fig 337. Lead jab parried on the inside.

Fig 338. Half beat bridge punch.

Fig 339. Lead straight as the pad man steps back.

the most important man in the class. A poor pad man means a poor workout so you must first learn to hold the gloves correctly.

There are two basic ways of holding the gloves. The first is known as the 'L' shape. For this, the pad man holds the gloves at a 90-degree angle to each other, allowing the trainer to check his partner's body mechanics and form. This set-up also lets you practise hand immobilization attacks and half-beat timing exercises (see Fig 334).

The second way of holding the gloves is known as the 'V', with palms facing outwards at a 45-degree angle.

The 'V' method can be used once the practitioner has developed good body mechanics and is ready for more explosive fast combinations that mimic the actual fight. It is also a great way to develop a strong penetrating straight blast using the wedge principle (see Fig 335).

A more advanced way of working the gloves is to have the pad man attacking as well as holding the targets. This makes the practitioner work his defensive parries, covers, evasion, footwork and timed hits. In fact, a good glove man can make the drill the next best thing to actual sparring (see Figs 336–339).

The Kick Shield

Although most kicks can be performed on the focus gloves, in order to develop real power in your kicks a much firmer target is required. Most kick shields are designed to absorb full-power kicks, allowing you to develop a deeper penetration without injuring the holder. Once you have developed kicks from a stationary position combine them with footwork skills, closing the gap from a distance. A more advanced drill is to have the shield holder take a step towards you so that you can develop the jarring effect of the stop-kicks (see Figs 340–342).

Fig 340. Partner holds kick shield.

Fig 341. Side kick.

Fig 342. Rear knee strike.

The Heavy Bag

The heavy bag is one of the best all-round conditioning tools available and does not require a training partner. Often beginners are too enthusiastic and will use relentless, uncontrollable swings when approaching the heavy bag for the first time so it is important to have some good basic mechanics laid down before working out on it. All the basic combinations can be practised on the bag and this is a good way to get lots of repetition of new combinations, ingraining them into the neuromuscular system. Always maintain good form and try to move around the bag using footwork. Remember the bag does not hit back, so you must maintain evasion skills as if you are fighting an opponent – in other words, 'keep moving'. Sometimes break the rhythm when working combinations on the bag by adding in pauses, feints, fakes and false hits. Negative shots can also be mixed in.

Fig 343. The heavy bag.

Try speed punch-out drills. Straight blast the heavy bag for 30 seconds then rest for 15 seconds – try this for several rounds for a great workout. You can also straight blast the heavy bag with full power, aiming to keep the bag out at an angle for a one-minute round. This is excellent resistance training and gives a devastating straight blast.

The same idea can be used with kicks. Using the ball of the foot, push-kick from the hip and alternate left and right kicks to keep the bag out at an angle for the duration of the round.

Single tools can be repeated out in tens, for example, fire ten jabs, ten rear straights and ten lead hooks. Make your own list of tools and drill them out. Try ten rear round kicks, ten lead thrust kicks and ten lead switch round kicks. This is a great conditioning workout. Make sure your heavy bag is indeed 'heavy' – a 'light' bag will swing too freely.

Fig 344. Close up of lead hook.

Fig 345. Inside biu-jee on the wooden dummy.

Fig 346. Trap and punch on the wooden dummy.

The Wooden Dummy

The wooden dummy is a training device from the Wing Chun system of gung fu that has been adopted by the Jeet Kune Do practitioner. In Jeet Kune Do the dummy is used to practise all of the hand immobilization tools, the bridge punches that simulate time-hits and low-line kicking.

The dummy is divided into the three areas of attack; high, middle and low. The high area has two arms protruding out at set angles, which allows for the correct working of the high-line tools. It has one mid-level arm to train mid-level defence and a branch from the mid to low area, which represents an opponent's lead leg.

The wooden dummy is a great device for forearm conditioning. The forearms should be able to withstand the impact of an opponent's arm when straight blasting or bridge punching.

The arms and frames of the dummy can also double up as a stretching frame, using the arms to rest the foot on whilst stretching out.

12 Final Note – Is Jeet Kune Do in Danger of Becoming a Lost Art?

Jeet Kune Do has its own look, which is distinctive from that of other martial arts. This sets it apart, and if it is to survive and retain its own identity, the structure must remain intact. Jeet Kune Do has a purposeful design, a seamless fitting-together of all its parts, and is about speed, efficiency and directness, keeping things as simple as possible in the most direct way.

Jeet Kune Do is not about taking the best from the martial arts world and making your own Jeet Kune Do. This requires several different structures that often will not fit together because of the conflicting purposes of design. The danger of adding to the structure is that it is easy to stray too far away from its design and purpose. It loses its directness and simplicity, until it is no longer Jeet Kune Do.

The core structure of Jeet Kune Do forms the basis of our martial art journey. If we are to flow naturally and intuitively in a fight, and 'let it happen', then the structure of Jeet Kune Do has to be internalized. This means many hours of refining it to make it your own. After years of refining this material, one starts to hack away the unessential, modifying and adjusting to find one's personal form. This becomes your own Jeet Kune Do, which has developed from the root structure and is built upon your own experiences of the art. To discover one's strengths and weaknesses one needs to be immersed in the art for a long time, and then one can start to adapt.

The spontaneous (or third) stage of cultivation is also known as the stage of freedom: to have the ability to adapt and fit in with an opponent requires you to have internalized the basic fundamentals of the art. The letting-go of techniques does not mean that you throw away all your have learned in order to start your journey; it simply means that you do not have to think about the technique. By emptying the mind of techniques, you are all techniques. Like water, formless and shapeless; if you put it into a vessel it becomes the vessel. Having no form is to have all forms.

If the Jeet Kune Do practitioner is to fit in with all opponents then it is important to research the latest trends in the martial arts and to keep up with the latest scientific training methods. Take, for example, the present trend in martial arts, which is grappling. If Jeet Kune Do covers the 'three ranges of combat' (long, medium and close), then all ranges need to be addressed. Close range entails grappling both standing and on the ground. If the Jeet Kune Do man is to fit in with a grappler he needs to understand his opponent's strengths and weaknesses as well as his own. It is no good taking the attitude of 'My stand-up is so good that I won't be taken to the ground.' This will probably lead to a rude awakening. It is far better to expect the possibility, to work out defences to the takedown and to be able to fight from the ground. Following the philosophical tenets of simple-direct and non-classical as the guide, researching other martial arts will allow us to adapt and modify techniques to the existing structure.

The only danger of adding to the structure of Jeet Kune Do is that it is easy to stray too far away from its design and purpose. If it loses its directness and simplicity, it will no longer be Jeet Kune Do.

Glossary: Terminology Used in Jeet Kune Do

Attack on completion Counter-attack as an opponent completes his attack

Attack on development Counter-attack in the midst of an opponent's attack

Attack on preparation Counter-attack as an opponent steps towards you

Bridging Cutting into an opponent's tool with a tool of your own

Bridging the gap Closing the fighting measure

Broken rhythm Pausing or stuttering a motion during a combination attack

Cadence Speed regulated to that of an opponent

Centre line Line that runs down the centre of the body

Compound attack Combination attack that starts with a feint

Dissolving Redirecting an opponent's energy

Drawing Leaving a line of attack open to facilitate a desired response

Economy of motion Using the most direct and efficient line of attack, thereby using minimum effort to get maximum effect

Evasion Movement to avoid an attack

Feinting Deceiving an opponent

Half beat An attack between two full beats

Probe An explorative movement

Reflex training Developing faster reflexes

Rhythm Grouping together of timed beats and parts of beats

Sensitivity Feeling an opponent's movement

Sticking energy Maintaining contact with an opponent's limbs

Stop-hit Intercepting an opponent

Tempo The speed of the beat

Tools Weapons of attack

Glossary: Chinese Terminology Used in Jeet Kune Do

Bai-jong Ready or on-guard stance
Biu-jee Finger jab
Biu-sau Forearm cover block
Bong-sau Wing arm deflection
Chi-sau Sticking hands
Chop-chuie Knuckle fist
Chung-chuie Front fist, lead straight
Da Strike
Dan-chi-sau Single hand sticking
Dok-sau Set attack and counter in chi-sau
Dum-tek Stomp kick
Fook-sau Bridging hand
Gin-lai Salute
Gor-sau Freestyle chi-sau
Gum-sau Pinning hand
Ha-pak High cross parry
Huen-sau Circling hand
Jau-sau Running hand
Jeung-sau Blending the position and changes in chi-sau
Jeet-tek Stop-kick
Jeet-kune Intercepting fist
Jik-chung-chuie Straight blast
Jik-tek Straight kick
Juk-tek Side kick
Jun Fan Bruce Lee's name
Jut-sau Jerking hand

Kwoon School
Leung-bye-muk Blindfold chi-sau
Lin-lap-sau Cross grabbing hand
Lin-sil-die-da Simultaneous parry and hit
Lop-sau Outside grabbing hand
Loy Inside
Mon-sau Inquisitive hand
Mook-Jong Wooden dummy
Nau-tek Hook kick
Noy Outside
Noy-pak/Loy-da Split entry
Pak-sau Slap hand
Ping-chuie Horizontal fist
Qua-chuie Backfist
Sat-sau Knife-hand strike
Seung-chi-sau Changing from position to position in chi-sau
Sifu Teacher, father
Si-gung Your teacher's teacher
Si-hing Your senior (male)
Si-ja Your senior (female)
Si-mo Wife of teacher
Sijo Founder of system
Soe-gerk Foot sweep
Sut Knee
Tan-sau Palm-up block
Whu-sau Protecting hand
Yu-bay Ready

Index